About the Author

Sharnae Smith is a barred attorney eight years into her career. After helping countless friends, relatives, and acquaintances strategize and start their own businesses, she is now proud to offer her consulting services to new and aspiring entrepreneurs, no matter where they are in the process off achieving self-employment and financial independence.

Sharnae was born and raised in the Washington, D.C. metropolitan area. She graduated from George Washington University with a B.A. in Political Science in 2007, and from the Campbell University School of Law in 2010. She became a solo practitioner in 2012 and complemented her business by working as an Adjunct Professor at the Community College of Baltimore County where she taught business law. Since then, she has worked for several law practices performing contract work and has maintained her practices in business law and estate planning. She has spread her wings by becoming a repeat entrepreneur, this time in the fields of consulting, publishing, and retail.

This book is the result of half a decade of hard work developing herself and her business, learning how to overcome obstacles, navigate the ups and downs of entrepreneurship, and make her mark on the world. To learn more about her and her project, visit sharnaesmith.com.

Mogul Moves: Practical Tips for Mastering Entrepreneurship

Published by **Smith Ventures, LLC.**
Bowie, MD USA

Mogul Moves: Practical Tips for Mastering Entrepreneurship

Sharnae Smith

For my family

Contents

Introduction

I wish I read a book like this when I first became an entrepreneur. By reading this book, you get to avoid the things I have learned the hard way, the common mistakes of early entrepreneurs, and the pitfalls that come early-on in journeys of entrepreneurship. In this introduction and in the following chapters, I use my story to describe the steps, or "moves," that *moguls* make in order to be successful in their businesses. These moves are relatable and practical, so much so that you can apply them to your life and businesses, starting right now! I will show you how making these moves in entrepreneurship will help you to achieve the levels of success that you desire.

"Entrepreneur" is a term used to describe someone who starts their own business. Those who are successful at as entrepreneurs are often referred to as "moguls" in their respective areas of business. You have heard of hip-hop moguls, media moguls, and fashion moguls; in every case, the word refers to people who have achieved a wide and often highly public level of success in their respective areas. When I think of a mogul, I think of someone who displays several crucial characteristics. These are: persistence and perseverance through the ups and downs of entrepreneurship; confidence in who they are and in their business strategies and approaches; and wide name- or brand-recognition. What I mean by "name recognition" is a situation where someone has reached such a high level in their field, thanks to their knowledge and ability to cultivate and develop their businesses, that other people emulate them, seeking to use them as models to achieve the same kind of success.

Moguls are not successful by accident, and regardless of what field they are in, they always possess the basic characteristics mentioned above. Developing those traits is not easy, and it can only happen as part of your personal journey through entrepreneurship. Everyone's journey starts differently, and without guidance, it can be hard to know what to do next. This book is here to help with just that problem. What I am going to do is tell you the key parts of my own story, pointing out, as I go, where I stepped wrong, what choices paid off in the end, and what skills and supports were needed to get through each stage of my development as an entrepreneur. My advice will be direct, in the form of explicit lessons, checklists, goals, and reflections. By taking you through my journey, I will be preparing you to set off on your own.

My journey to entrepreneurship started much earlier than I realized, and was heavily influenced by where I grew up. As a Prince George's County, Maryland girl born in the District of Columbia, I have been surrounded by excellence all my life. I was born the second of four girls in a household where there was never a dull moment. Ours was something of a traditional home; my father was the breadwinner and my mother was a home-maker and educator. Dad worked long hours, and some days we would only see him before we left for school, because we were asleep by the time he got home. I remember staring at his schedule where it was posted on the refrigerator door, memorizing the days he was going to be off work so that I would know when to expect him home. It was always such a treat to see his car in front of the house when we got back from school.

My mother, on the other hand, was always around. She was at home with us during the day, brought all of us to our extra-curricular activities and practices, and took on shifts as a substitute teacher at our schools. She was never far away.

The windows of the house were always open to "air out the house" as dad would say. He was a bit "type A," and what he really meant was that he was cleaning the house again, and needed to let out the strong smell of the cleaning chemicals.

Prince George's County, both then and now, was the wealthiest African American county in the United States of America. To the world, we fit the narrative of the successful Prince George's County middle-class black family. We drove Lexus and Acura vehicles and lived in good neighborhoods. But behind closed doors, we were struggling. We were a product of our environment, one where financial literacy was not taught and living above your means was the thing to do. And so, despite the cars we drove and the zip codes we lived in, I know what it feels like to depend on the local church's food pantry for food, to go without hot water, and to live without basic necessities. With all that said, the fact that our family has done as well as it has is a testament to the strength of our faith and perseverance.

I was fortunate to have a wonderful education, both at home and at school. I attended a public school, but I had some wonderful teachers there who made education fun and easy for me to enjoy. In fact, my siblings and I loved to learn so much that we would role-play "school" at home. One of us would be the teacher, the rest of us would be the students. We would practice math, spelling, writing, and just about anything else we wanted. Of course, my mother had no objections, and she would let us play this way for hours.

I remember being terribly upset when, at nine years old, I had the flu and had to miss school. Education was a passion of mine, along with making good grades. This was so much the case that when I got my first "B" on a report card, my mother had to enlist the school counselor to help me work through my emotional reaction. I was devastated. I have come a long way since that moment, but my passion for education has followed me into adulthood.

I would go on to graduate from George Washington University with a bachelor's degree in political science, and then to earn my juris doctor degree from Campbell Law School. In other words, my educational journey was a long one. It has turned out to be nothing at all, though, compared to the journey I would ultimately take in my path to successful entrepreneurship.

I believe that entrepreneurship chose me. It was not a childhood dream of mine, and at the beginning, it was something I was forced into doing in order to survive. Once I became an entrepreneur, I found that survival as a business owner was even harder than survival as an unemployed job-seeker. I gave up for a while, and it has taken time for me to find my way back to entrepreneurship. This whole part of my journey started when I finished law school and entered the job market for the first time.

In 2010, I graduated law school and passed the Maryland State bar exam on my first try. Now, when I started law school career, my plan was the same as that of most law students. One: finish school. Two: land a judicial clerkship at a local courthouse in my home state. And three: move on to a job at a law firm paying the big bucks – and hopefully doing something I loved.

That whole plan vanished when an economic recession swept through the United States, sending the whole legal field into limbo. First-year lawyers were being laid off in favor of older attorneys' self-entitlement to their bonuses. Judicial clerks were being allowed to serve for two years instead of the usual one, because judges pitied the clerks' situations. Many of them had full-time jobs lined up at firms for after their clerkships were slated to end, only to find their job offers rescinded at the height of the recession.

And then there were us, the entire population of 2010 law-school graduates. We entered a market badly over-saturated with lawyers. Demand had run dry when it came to legal services, and there was very little work available to most of us. I was offered part-time positions at $20,000 per year, and full time at $30,000. For qualified legal work in the Washington, D.C. metropolitan area, those offers were, honestly, outrageous. If you know anything about what lawyers tend to make — especially in metro areas — then your jaw is probably still on the floor. I know what this is making you think: "That cannot be real life!" Oh, but it was. It was MY life, and the life of almost every other law student who graduated that year.

I landed my first position as a seasonal worker at a nearby retail store. At this point, I was as far from my planned-out future as I could possibly have been. I did what I could: only a few months later, I left my job, formed a limited liability company, and began a solo law practice. Over that next year, I built up my practice until I was fully self-sufficient and self-employed.

Let me just clarify and emphasize what I am trying to relay to you: <u>less than a year out law school, and months after being sworn in to the</u>

local bar, I was working full-time for <u>MYSELF</u>! Can you believe that? Looking back, it was a bold move on my part. It was also one that I have taken advantage of. I still have my law firm, and I am also running several other businesses.

So, why did I make that choice? Why did I become an entrepreneur? This is a question I still ask myself, when work is not as plentiful and the times get hard. Some of my original reasons still stand, including the desire to take my destiny into my own hands, the need to be able to build wealth on my own terms, and not wanting to allow corporate America to determine whether I could provide for myself or not.

In the time since then, I have found additional reasons that make being an entrepreneur near and dear to me. Generational wealth is the most important of them. Coming from a family who did not have much by way of financial resources when I was growing up, I saw how important financial literacy and wealth-building are. Now, I have equipped myself with the tools to create those conditions on my own, and I want to be able to share them with others. Wealth starts with your mindset, so if I can help inspire others, changing their minds about the feasibility of accumulating generational wealth, I will be satisfied with a job well done. Additionally, when I have a family of my own someday, I want to be able to call my own shots. I want not to be controlled by student debt, and I want to pass what I have learned on down to my family and loved ones. Financial freedom and wealth both for myself and for my legacy is the ultimate goal of the work I am doing now.

I am writing this book because I want you to know that you do not have to come from money to build and create wealth. I want people to understand that there is a specific mindset that you can tap into, and specific actions that you can take, to help you become whatever type of *mogul* you aspire to be. If you are the kind of person who is reading this book, then there is a *mogul* inside of you waiting to be unleashed. You have gifts, you have talents, you have education, you have things that only you can do and a perspective that only you can bring to the world. I want to show you how to understand your own potential and use it to your advantage.

As a second-time business owner and evolving entrepreneur, I am here to tell you that with faith, hope, the right attitude, and the right work ethic you can and will become something greater than you could ever imagine. I had to walk away from my first business for a while, and I learned many lessons from that part of my journey. These days, I am actively running my second business and building toward a time when I can leave my full-time job to work exclusively for myself again.

Stick with me in the first chapter as I tell you a bit more of my personal story. Many of the things I learned early-on about finding success as a rising mogul came from details of my own journey, which is why my advice to you will be given through the medium of autobiography. We are all far more similar than we are different, and you will probably notice similarities between my story and yours. I will also refer back to some of these stories later on in the book. This journey has been a rollercoaster, but it is one that I am choosing to stay on, and one that I hope you will take the leap of faith to jump onto as well!

Chapter 1. My Story

The bar exam

It was the summer of 2010, and I was spending both my days and my nights studying for the bar exam in July. I opted to hand-write my exam, all twelve hours of it, instead of taking it electronically. I knew that I processed my thoughts better that way, and that the exam would require all of my abilities.

(Quick aside here. I know that you are probably thinking, "Who is crazy enough to write out a twelve-hour exam when they could type it instead?" Well, if you were asking me, I would raise my hand. I learned during law school that I am a better test-taker when I write my answers out with a pen. During my first semester, I took all of my final exams on the computer, even though I took hand-written notes in class, and my grades reflected the sudden shift in format—Christmas break was not much fun once I got them back. In the second semester, when I decided to write my exams by hand, my grades increased by ten or twenty points in just about every class. This is a basic *mogul move*: use your strengths to your advantage. When you are in school, know your learning style! Anyway, back to the story.)

I prepared for the state bar exam by taking a bar preparation course that was hailed as the best in the state. In the course, we had several hours of homework to do every day. I did test questions and timed myself as I took them, writing for hours at a time. After the first several weeks, I noticed that the curriculum the course used was only helping me to get to where I needed to be for some parts of the exam. I decided to tailor the material they gave us to suit my personal test-prep needs. I set aside the study schedule they gave us, and devoted my time only to the topics I knew the least about, and for which my writing was least fluid. I stopped wasting time on questions I was already prepared for. In education and in the office, remember that the goal is always to work smarter, not just harder.

I studied literally day and night. Family members would quiz me with index cards I made, matching legal terms with their definitions or elements. I frequented every Panera Bread and Barnes and Noble in a 55-mile radius. My pattern was to set up in the morning, alone or with a study group, and stay until late in the evening. More often than not, I studied from sun up to sun down, sometimes catching a nap in between. I spent the Fourth of July studying. On my mother's birthday, I studied. I think you get the point. I was one hundred percent committed to passing the bar, and that meant LOTS of studying.

The morning of the exam came along, and I was unexpectedly sick. And yet, of course, there was nothing to be done: I knew I had to take the exam. There was no turning back! My mother drove me to the test site, and sat outside praying for me the entire time. To understand the weight and impact of what she was doing, you need to know that just two months earlier, she was ill enough herself to be on her death bed. That story is for another day; what matters here is that I was helped through the bar by an amazing support system (a topic we will return to in Chapter Ten) and also, of course, that it had not always been easy to stay focused over the course of that summer.

So: the exam. I recall walking in and sitting down inside a brightly lit building at the Timonium Fairgrounds, in Maryland. At the time, it reminded me of the cafeteria scene in that 90s movie *Matilda*, where droves of children sit around plastic tables watching one kid being forced to eat a whole chocolate cake up on stage. The only real difference, I felt, was that there was nothing sweet in my situation. Daunting.

I was seated at a very thin table with barely enough space to fit all my pencils. I was surrounded by aspiring lawyers, and all of our fates would soon be decided by one exam and *twelve* grueling hours.

Once we were allowed to begin the test, I opened my text booklet and looked at the first essay question. I had absolutely no idea as to what the answer to that question was. I was prepared for this kind of situation, though. I had spent months, and, before that, years of school, conditioning myself to take this exam. I knew that I could not afford to allow panic to overcome me. I knew that if I did not overcome the frustration of that first, impossible question, I would lose my nerve and my focus and fail the entire exam. So, I buckled down. I took my best shot at a reasonable answer and moved on.

The second question was mental and emotional redemption. I knew the answer, I would have known the answer in my sleep. That restored some of my confidence, but I was still aware that getting hung up on how I was doing would only hurt my performance. I had to finish the exam.

Twelve hours later, I ran out of time on the very last essay question, which was worth twice as much as any of the others. Needless to say, I was not very confident in my results.

My first job, and bar scores revealed

The state of Maryland takes four months to score their bar exam. I would not find out whether I passed until November of 2010. In the meantime, having not yet passed the bar, I could not practice as an attorney. I needed to support myself, though, so I applied to all kinds of positions. The first one I landed was a seasonal position at a Banana Republic in a local mall. Naturally, this was a huge disappointment. I had been hoping to be called back by one of the hundreds of legal positions I had applied to. But, no such luck.

I worked as many hours as I could at Banana Republic. I spent early mornings folding shirts and hanging clothes. I worked the overnight shift on Black Friday, and worked long hours on Christmas. I hoped that by the end of the season, I would have positive results on my exam. I also continued to work towards landing a position in the legal field.

Time passed. On the day that results for the bar exam were scheduled to be posted, I had to go to work. (Insert eye roll here.) Now, the bar exam is graded anonymously, so each test-taker is assigned an identifying number that they can use to anonymously check their exam results. The results were posted online at 3:00 in the afternoon. One number after another would be listed, and if yours was not among them, you had not passed. This setup gave me flashbacks to dance club tryouts when I was in Middle School, walking up to a white piece of paper pinned to a board on the wall, PRAYING my name was on the list. Trembling steps, rapid heartbeat, throat feeling like I had swallowed a goat, all of that. With this in mind, for the sake of my sanity, I left my test number at home with relatives. I asked them to check the results for me, both because I would be working and because I was just too terrified to look myself. I specifically told my family to wait until I got off work to call me with the results. In true family fashion, they did not listen.

I spent that day working the register, which meant that I was near the phone. In the middle of the afternoon, it began to ring. I answered and heard a voice on the other end saying, "May I speak to Sharnae Smith, please?" I recognized the voice as my younger sister's. A little incensed and a lot excited, I responded, "Didn't I tell you not to call me at work with the results?"

But right then, my entire family proceeded to scream, "YOU PASSED!" I heard a roar of voices in the background, screaming, clapping, and yelling. I found myself screaming and yelling with them. Tears welled up in my eyes, just because I screamed so long and so hard that my body did not know what to do with itself. Customers started looked at me strangely, and I got off of the phone in a hurry. I explained what was happening, first to the customers and then to my co-workers, over the radio. I was elated! For a brief moment, I was able to celebrate what I had worked so hard for: the accomplishment of a major goal, thanks to my bone-deep commitment to the process of seeing it through. Through all of the ups and downs, I had stuck with it, and now, in the middle of the afternoon in a Banana Republic, I had made it. In that moment, I celebrated with a pure, wild joy unclouded by employment failure, and it was glorious!

I GOT A JOB!

Once I was sworn in to the state bar as a lawyer, I was given a free subscription to the state bar association. I was new, I was green, I was excited to get to work! I did not stop to think about business etiquette, professional rules the bar association might have in place, or other related considerations.

I decided to take a direct approach: I sent out an email on the state bar's listserv for local attorneys, asking about employment opportunities. It went to thousands of attorneys. Every single potential colleague in the immediate area. I included my resume, and asked whether anyone might consider hiring a new attorney, or if they knew someone who was looking for help.

Deafening silence. Just one attorney was kind enough to respond. They told me that soliciting jobs on the professional listserv was against the rules, but, impressed that I "had the balls to do it," they invited me to come down and interview for a part-time position at their law firm.

I had never felt like such an idiot. The first major mistake I made as a new attorney had been to beg for a job in a setting where it was against the rules to do so. But then, I got what I wanted. So much for list serve etiquette! The end result of my mistake was that I attained a part-time position as an associate attorney, working at a family law firm about an hour and a half away from my home.

A part-time position was not what I was looking for, of course. So right then, even as I was just entering the legal world, I started setting up my own law practice. This went on while I worked in that first position and while I held several different positions over the subsequent few years. This was my first leap into the world of entrepreneurship: just a couple of months into my legal employment journey, I filed my Articles of Organization to form my own limited liability company, officially establishing my solo legal practice. Crucially, this was not my only venture; I did it while also working as an associate attorney at a small law firm.

After that period, I moved into contract work. I took on document review jobs for huge law firms in the District of Columbia. Document review is a process that requires attorneys to read over documents in anticipation of a law suit, or as part of a lawsuit that is already in progress. Thousands, and sometimes hundreds of thousands of documents are reviewed for each case. It required long hours on the job, sometimes including fourteen-hour days, and the contract positions could end at any time. Any time a lawsuit reached a settlement, the contract related to it would end, many times without meaningful prior notice for the contract employees.

Building my practice took a long time, and I was not doing contract work for all of it. This meant that I was effectively without a job during periods without document review work. Being unemployed as an attorney was mentally, emotionally, and financially tough. I had spent so many years in college and law school, only to find myself feeling like a total failure. It was hardly any better during the periods when I was formally employed by contract, because I had no way of knowing when my next contract would start. Nor did I ever have any assurance that an active contract would not abruptly end. The uncertainty built up over time, leaving me in a constant state of fear and anxiety.

The positions for attorney contract work would often be advertised with projected time frames that the job would last for. The postings would often look like this:

> BIGA Company is staffing a document review beginning tomorrow. If you are interested, please see the details below:
>
> Start date: Tomorrow
> Anticipated Duration: Two weeks to one year
> Pay rate: $30 per hour; 1.5 for OT
> DC bar required: Yes
> Location: Metro Center

Sometimes, having been hired for a position like this, I would show up for the first day of work and immediately be told to go home. The volatility of attorney contract work is just that great. Cases can be settled prior to a lawsuit even being filed, or right after a lawsuit begins. When that happened, the contract would be canceled, leaving all of the new hires effectively unemployed again.

Sometimes new projects would be available shortly after the previous one ended or was cancelled, and other times there would be long dry spells, with no contract work available for months.

Taken all together, these working conditions left me in a constant state of fear and anxiety, never knowing whether I would still have employment when I woke up the next day.

After years of these rapid, hard-to-bear ups and downs, I decided that there was only one reasonable course of action: to take my destiny into my own hands. I decided to work for myself on a full-time basis. I knew that self-employment, too, could be unpredictable, but I thought, "how bad could it really be?" As it turned out, I was not quite prepared for the answer to that question.

How bad could it really be? My first year in business

When I decided to become a full-time entrepreneur, I already had my own business formally set up. About a year earlier, as a young lawyer almost fresh out of law school, I knew everything I needed to do in order to start a limited liability company. So, while I held my first legal position as a part-time associate attorney, I filed my Articles of Organization and started my own solo law practice. At that time, I was not yet ready to dive into self-employment, but I knew that I would want to work for myself in some capacity at some point. My thought, initially, was to do a limited amount of business on the side to complement the income from my other job, because I was only working part-time.

That plan changed quickly when, later on during that first year as a lawyer, I found myself in and out of employment. Early in 2012, I stopped taking on contract-based document review jobs and began to work for myself on a full-time basis, operating a general law practice as a solo practitioner.

I accepted jobs from just about anyone who walked through my door, but most of my cases were family and criminal law. I dealt with foreclosure protection, speeding ticket defense, declarations of bankruptcy, and unemployment insurance. For each new kind of case, I had to get up to speed very quickly with case law in the relevant area. That kind of competency is a MUST in legal practice. You need it to be able to do the job well, on top of which you can be sued for malpractice if you are practicing incompetently in a legal area. So early on, much of my time was spent reading and learning as much as I could about the new areas of law that I was working with in-depth for the first time.

I recall it being a grueling year. As a new solo practitioner with no savings, no employees, no business credit, no bookkeeper, and no marketing system to help bring in new clients, I was forced to wear all of those hats myself. I found my first client through a word of mouth referral from a law school classmate. That client kept me BUSY. If having only one child support case could have paid all the bills, I would still be operating my practice full-time. Instead, it was a lot of work without the pay to match.

To help grow my business, I wrote articles in local online newspapers, taught courses at local community centers, started a blog, and joined referral lists for the local bar associations. One by one, clients were coming in. It felt good to see my efforts paying off. That year I had about a dozen clients. That is not a huge number, even for a private practice, so I took on additional work as well, teaching business law for paralegals as an adjunct professor at a local community college.

This is what it means to be a solo legal practitioner with no one working for you: I was responsible for correspondence with opposing counsel or opposing parties who represented themselves; correspondence with judges and trustees; client intake and correspondence; legal research and writing, including drafting and filing motions, pleas, and any paperwork related to the cases; bookkeeping; hiring service processors; marketing; representing clients in court representation; and a long list of other tasks.

On top of all that, I was not sleeping well. I was terrified of making a mistake and being sued for malpractice, and I would often wake up suddenly in the middle of the night with thoughts about a case. I would get out of bed to conduct research on the ideas I had come up with, and usually I could not fall back asleep. I was in the middle of my own personal horror story, complete with cold sweats and endless self-doubt. Needless to say, it was tiring. I burned out more times than I would like to admit, and I did not feel that the amount of energy that I was putting into building the business was producing the results I needed to be able to stick with it long-term. In addition to bills and operating costs, my student loans were playing the capitalization game, and I was losing.

(When I say, "the capitalization game," I am referring to a practice financial companies use to increase the balance on a loan that you owe them. If the amount you are paying on your loan does not cover the amount of interest it is accruing, the company often reserves the right to add that outstanding interest to the balance of your loan after a certain amount of time. This increases the base amount of your loan and causes you to both owe more and pay more over time.)

With so much weighing me down, I had to take a detour on the road to success as an entrepreneur. I decided to close up shop and get a job working for someone else.

Commitment to self-employment

Working for someone else for a while seemed like the best option for me at that time. Standard employment offered me steady income, health benefits, no personal liability in legal practice, and, most importantly, my sanity. From 2013 through 2016, I maintained my own legal practice on a part-time basis as I worked full-time in other positions. I knew that I did not want to give up on the goal of working for myself, but it was not feasible to pursue it directly for a while.

I worked in several capacities during that period, many of which included attorney contract work, performing document review. I did that exclusively from the beginning of 2013 through the end of 2014, when I was able to secure a position in the general counsel's office of a city government agency. For the next year, I supported the attorneys in that office in representing the government against lawsuits filed by citizens. Then, at the end of 2015, I was able to secure a full-time position at the state government level, facilitating negotiations between employees and government agencies. I also coordinated the mediation program for the entire state government. At the end of 2016, I moved on to an employee relations position, working for the federal government.

All of these jobs shared the downside that I was not working for myself. Working full-time for someone else left me without the time that I felt I needed to become successful on my own. I would often come home too tired to work or engage with prospective clients, and I knew that if I really wanted to pursue entrepreneurship, I would need to figure out a different arrangement.

More than that, I have never liked working for someone else. It was always difficult being told what to do and when to do it. It was difficult having to compete for raises, and sometimes not getting them thanks to obscure agency rules, despite being more than qualified to receive one. In other words, it was difficult not being in control of my own destiny. I knew that I could only live that way for so long before deciding to build my own empire and continue my journey to PERMANENT full-time entrepreneurship.

During the four years from 2013 to 2016, even though I only practiced out of my solo law firm on a part-time basis, I brainstormed and formulated several other potential business models. When enough time had gone by, I decided that it was time to launch back out into entrepreneurship, this time on my own terms and much more prepared.

In May of 2017 I decided to launch my own consulting company, focused on wealth-building and wealth-protection achieved through estate planning and business development. At the time of writing, I am still in the midst of my journey to full-time self-employment and have been making major headway.

Since making the decision to launch my new business, I have been kept busy by speaking engagements and connecting with some amazing entrepreneurs who have been in this business for decades now. They are all *moguls*, successful in their own right in their respective fields. Thanks to their wisdom and insight, and because this is my second go-round with entrepreneurship, I am much better equipped with what I need to succeed.

And that is what I want to share with you here. With the years of experience I have had in my private law practice, and now in my new business venture, I have so much I want to tell you, so much to share that will help you on your own journey to success in business. This book will give you practical advice and tips on how to be successful in entrepreneurship and become a *mogul* in your own right. My hope is that it helps you understand what you need to do, and the characteristics and environments you will need to seek out, in order to build and run a successful business. Get a pen and some paper and take notes as you read. Each of the subsequent chapters highlights key information that you will want to keep with you on your journey.

Before you move on to the next chapter, I want you to answer the questions below. Then, when you have finished reading the book, I want you to come back to your answers and compare your new, more educated perspective with what you wrote here, at the very beginning.

Reflect and Write

What do you hope to learn from reading this book?

What are some characteristics you think you need when starting a business?

What are some characteristics you think you will need to keep the business up and going?

Chapter 2. Know Who You Are

Moguls know exactly who they are and are not
afraid to reinvent and rebrand themselves as they
evolve.

In this chapter, I am going to use my story to show you how I developed

my personal business identity, so that you can use my experiences and

advice to guide you in learning yours. I will tell you the story of how I

came to learn who I am. As I do, I will build on the story to show you

how that knowledge then led me to what I was passionate about. I will

connect those elements to show you that learning about yourself is the

foundation of your business identity. This is something that *moguls*

understand well.

My journey to knowing who I am really started back in college, but I

am going to give you some historical background that leads up to that

point. We will start with my very first career aspirations.

Who are you?

> Here's where I am these days. I'm thirty-two and I
> don't know what I want to be "when I grow up."
> I've grown to love and accept that. But I do know
> *who* I want to be. I just want to be me.

> Whereas, twenty-five years ago, this is where my
> seven-year-old self was at: "When I grow up, I
> want to be a gospel singer for God's word."

Let me set the stage. It was Christmas in 1992, the cameras were rolling,

and we were all asked what we wanted to be when we grew up. Two of

my classmates said "doctor," but I said that I wanted to be a gospel

singer. Now, I know that I gave the CHURCHIEST answer known to

mankind, but I did not say that because giving a churchy answer was my

goal. I said it because I knew that singing was something I loved,

something that brought me joy, and something that I happened to be

pretty good at. As I got older, that passion never left me, but I ultimately

chose a direction that involved no creativity. I did not do this entirely by

my own free choice; I was molded to pursue a high-paying career, at the

expense of what really mattered to me.

As children, most of us were taught that we can grow up to be

whatever we want to be. But our parents and teachers did not respond equally well to all of our wants, wishes, and dreams. Parents are proud when their little girl says she wants to be a lawyer, but quiet when she says she wants to become an artist. We are groomed at young ages to start thinking about what we want to become, not as a person, but in our careers. We are asked countless times, "what do you want to be when you grow up?" And under the influence of parental attitudes and values, some of us chose things we genuinely loved, but most of us chose what we thought were glamorous, worthwhile careers. You know, the widely rehearsed and recited ones that every child knows their parents would be proud of them for picking. The ones you are almost boxed in to saying: doctor, lawyer, firefighter, police officer, teacher. We are constantly pushed and steered to become one those things.

Very rarely does someone attend college and graduate with a degree that they will ultimately use in the job market or in their life's work. Why is this? Fundamentally, it is because at college-age we lack a clear understanding of who we are. If we knew more about who we wanted to be, or at least had a better understanding of ourselves, we would be equipped to make better decisions, at younger ages, to more positively shape our own futures.

Do you know who does not have that problem? *Moguls.* One of their defining features is that they possess absolutely certain knowledge of who they are. Most have gone through a journey of self-discovery that has launched them into the area where they currently thrive. As a result, they are self- assured. Confident. They are sure of who they are, and what they are going to do with that knowledge. They are not afraid to take risks.

College and identity crisis

When I started college as a student at Towson University, I came in with my intention to study pre-med already declared. I thought medicine was what I wanted to do. I knew I was smart enough for it, and it seemed like a glamorous career. Who dislikes the thought of helping people and saving lives? I was so sure of this decision that I registered as a Biology major. All of that changed when I found out that, were I to become a physician, I would have to deal with the bodily fluids of strangers, day in and day out. One semester in to college, I changed my major to "undecided."

In my heart, I felt lost. If I was not going into medicine, what else would I do? The only thing that I knew I loved was dancing. I had been formally trained in different types of dance on and off throughout my life, and I liked the idea of pursuing it as a career. So, I went on to declare myself to be a dance major.

Changing my major was one of the scariest things I had ever done. In my family, changing your major was a cardinal sin. My older sister chose her major, and stuck with it. She and I used to joke about serial major-changers, the people who change majors like they change their underwear. The ones who are career undergraduate students, often overstaying the four-year timeframe by several years. Changing my major felt like joining that club. The sense of shame I felt was very real and very intense. This kind of shame is how many of us end up limiting our own career choices and potential. Our own expectations, and those of the people around us, frequently push us toward just few career options. In changing my major, I felt like I had disappointed everyone, including myself. Up until then, when I had set out to do something, I stuck with it; this time, things were different. Change was needed, and change came, but it made me feel terrible.

It also was not easy. The dance department at Towson was very competitive to enter. You had to audition, and if you were accepted, you joined a strenuous program that many students did not make it through. I had been taking dance classes as electives there, and told some of my instructors that I wanted to change my major to dance. Their reaction was tentative. For instance, one of them encouraged me to attend some of the upper-level dance courses to see how well I could "hang in there" with the intensity of their exercises. I took one of the upper-level ballet classes, and all I need to tell you is that it was brutal. It was the hardest ballet class I ever took. I could barely walk for the rest of the day, and my sore muscles had me doing a weird, slew-footed stride. It was the only way I could get my hips not to yell at me for putting them through an experience that turned out to be torture. The best I could do was to fake a normal walk until I got back to my dorm room.

Later, I took an upper-level modern dance course. Modern dance was my thing. I did much better that time around, but I still felt discouraged about joining the program. Between the ballet and modern classes, I had seen that I was not as good as many of the other students, and that my training needed a lot of work. I could also see that I was far from the weakest student in either class, but this did little to encourage me. Nor did it feel very helpful when one of the professors told me that I was stronger than some of the other students. My best guess, then and now, is that they said that to encourage me. I think they wanted me to reason that if there was a person already there who was not as good as I was, might I not have been able to audition successfully and make it into the program? I might have. But I would never have the chance to find out.

Instead, I was pressured by authority figures in my life to choose a major that would lead me toward a career that would make a lot of money. I was told that I should not pursue dance seriously both because it is a hard field to make it in in general, and because my short, thick stature would cost me too many professional opportunities. I was told that dance might work as a backup plan, but never as my main plan. The issue with that advice was that there was no dance minor at Towson; dance was all or nothing.

With all of those considerations on my mind, I decided that I would change my major again! I settled for political science this time. I had been told that I would make a great lawyer, and that was the most lawyerly major I could think of. The only courses in the program that I enjoyed were the ones on international law; domestic United States politics did not interest me.

Even with this new plan, I got plenty of unhelpful commentary. Several people tried to talk me out of becoming an attorney because of the amount of reading and writing it involves, but I felt almost trapped at that point. I did not feel that I had much of a choice, because my attempts to explore other options had not gone well. I had felt forbidden to pursue dance, and medicine did not end up working out for me. That had been extremely discouraging, because medicine had seemed like such a sure thing. Science and medicine were the subjects I knew best and did best at, going into college, and I had gravitated to them in my grade school years. Whereas I had been made to feel that becoming a dancer was too risky, my interest there had not met with any acceptance, and there was no way to make it a backup option at Towson. So, I decided to press on and become a lawyer.

I started looking into the areas of law that I thought might interest me. I have always been a compassionate person, so I initially wanted to become an attorney who advocated for domestic violence victims. As I went on through my journey, the legal area I wanted to focus on changed many times.

Where was I going with this new career focus? I had no idea. I graduated college and headed to law school feeling almost as lost and confused as I was when I changed my major for the first time. I was good at faking confidence, and everyone thought I had it together, but the truth was just the opposite and fake confidence is no help at all. I was on a career path that I had barely chosen for myself, seeing as the pressure from those around me was by far the biggest factor in my decision. I was certainly "living the life," but not as myself.

The awesome thing about life is that over time, if you pay attention, you will find that everything you needed was already there within you. In my case, it took me some time to realize that, and to figure out who I was and who I wanted to be. Even with the detours I had to take during college, once I started on my journey to self-discovery, everything gradually started to make sense and fall into place. Law school was an expensive way to learn more about myself, and it required lots of self-reflection and self-acceptance along the way. But ultimately, it helped me to become who I truly am, and to live a life actively chosen by *me*, and no one else.

So, who am I?

I am many things. I am creative, inventive, artistic, musical, spiritual, intelligent, and too big and complex to be placed into any box. One of the best things I have learned from my journey is that I can choose to be more than one thing, or good at more than one thing. You can be all the different things that you are. What makes you different is the combination of talents, abilities, and experiences that you embody, not just the one that you can sell most easily. That whole combination is your brand. Those unique parts of you are the puzzle pieces to who you are, and without any one of them, you are not yourself.

After my first year of private practice, and after going back to work for other people, I gave myself a chance to explore my options. What did that look like for me? I took piano lessons, became a Zumba instructor, became the co-leader of a youth ministry at church, made myself a second-time business owner, and more. Of course, doing all of those things at once was tiring. I can see why many people choose to focus on one thing, or just a few things, but I am not many people. I am my own, unique self. And personally, I had to go through all of that to enjoy the fullness of who I am, and to set myself on the right direction for where I wanted to go, in life and in business.

Through that period of discovery, I was able to learn who I was, and to accept was I learned. Life opened up to me. I found that I did not need to try to be anyone else. I did not have to accept others' opinions about what I should do, or who I should be. By making space to consider the roads that were open to me, I got to choose my path for myself.

As I was preparing to get more serious about my dive into entrepreneurship for the second time, I chose to minimize what I was doing. I gave up piano lessons temporarily, let my Zumba license expire, and took a break from ministry so that I could focus on building my business. I did those things, not because I had to, but because I understood the importance of prioritizing. I still made time for the things that made me come alive, and was intentional about doing them all. I still practice the piano, and have my own personal dance fests. But I fit them in around the edges of my days now. As a committed entrepreneur, my time and resources are poured into my new businesses.

Identity defines your business

Here is where my story starts producing important lessons for you, the reader and entrepreneur. Starting my second business with full awareness of who I am was very helpful when it came time for me to create an identity for my business. Your business's identity is its brand. Every business has one, whether or not it is unique. The distinctiveness of your business's identity will help you to stand out among other businesses selling the same product or service, so getting it right is vital.

I named my business after me this time. Sharnae Smith. My goal was to move into consulting and speaking, and away from providing legal services, so I avoided branding myself with a name that sounded like it might belong to a law firm. Instead, I made it a representation of myself. It was logical for me to use just my name as my brand, and it helps that my first name is unique.

They next challenge you will face is coming up with a short tagline for your business. This is something I initially struggled with; being able to define your business in just a few words is difficult, especially when you offer such a variety of services. This task has become even more difficult recently, as your tagline needs to be able to define your business in a way that stands out on social media platforms. In my case, practically everyone online is a consultant or speaker, so the challenge was particularly daunting. (One thing to remember is that once you have your business name, you can work on these details later if the solutions do not present themselves right away.) Knowing your identity as a person will drive identity-formation of the business you want to start, and that in turn will drive the identity of your brand and everything that goes along with it.

Knowing your business identity will also help you identify who your target audience is. If you have any familiarity with entrepreneurship, you know that clearly delineating your target audience is key to your business's long-term success. Your target audience is who your products or services are geared toward. These are the people you want to be drawn to, or who you want to feel a need for your product or service.

Always remember that you are selling yourself far more than you are selling your product or service. Your clients will choose you on the basis of your brand and identity long before they know what you can offer them. Identify who you are, and you are well on your way.

Reflect and Write

Who are you?

What did you want to be as a kid?

What passions have you let go or not cultivated because of life experiences?

What is your business identity?

Chapter 3. Believe in Yourself

Believe in yourself and your products.

Have you ever started a business and felt that the services you were offering or the products you were selling were not good enough? Have you ever thought to yourself that you were not qualified to do the work you had chosen? Have you ever thought there were too many people doing the very thing that you want to do? Have you ever thought to yourself, "what's the point of trying when it is not going to work out anyways?" If you have, you are totally normal!

The truth is, every entrepreneur has had these thoughts; what matters is what you do with them. *Moguls* have mastered the art of believing in themselves, and they only work with, and represent, the services and products that they believe in.

When I first started my law practice, I did it to survive. I was less aware of the competition I was up against than I was of the fact that I just needed to earn some money. What I discovered was that in some ways, I had to fake it until I made it. I had to quickly become competent in every area of law that a client needed help with. My first client was referred to me by a law-school classmate. A client of his had a nephew in my local area who needed a family lawyer, and family law just so happened to be one of the areas I was working to become specialized in. It was only once I had that first contract, and I was working hard to grow my client base, I realized how saturated with lawyers my area was, and how difficult it was going to be to get enough business. Being in a suburb of Washington, D.C., there were lawyers and law practices everywhere. In this kind of situation, there is only so much you can do. Your only real option is to find unusual ways to make yourself stand out from the crowd.

In the first chapter, I mentioned a few of my efforts to distinguish myself. I am going to re-iterate some of those points for your recollection, now that you know more about their purpose in this story.

To help get the word out about my business, I began writing articles for the local online newspaper. I was contacted by one city to teach legal information courses to their residents as a part-time city employee. I registered with two nonprofit organizations to assist low-income individuals with their family law cases. I became a member of the local and state bar associations, and joined their referral lists. These efforts all took up valuable time, energy, and focus, and yielded mixed results.

I received a few cases from people who read my articles in the online newspaper, but the majority of my clientele came from word of mouth. And they were not enough to keep me afloat, so despite everything I was doing, I was still not receiving the quantity of clientele I needed to sustain both the firm and my sanity. To compound the problem, I found myself encountering the pitfalls of being self-employed for the first time. Any small business owner or freelancer will run into situations where their clients do not pay on time. That happened to me more than once. I also did many favors for family and friends, which often ended up being unpaid. Situations like these can leave you feeling taken advantage of, and, even worse, feeling that your work was not worth paying for. I knew that was not true—I knew my work was good—but even so it was difficult not to ruminate on all the possible reasons why someone might not pay me for my hard work.

Another problem with being self-employed is dealing with overhead. When you run a law practice, there are things you have to do, just by virtue of the nature of the profession, that make your day busier. Corresponding with opposing counsel, filing cases in person, corresponding with clerks in the court to ensure that your paperwork was received and that the judge has looked it over, corresponding with the same clerks all over again to make sure the court did not *lose* your paperwork (this took an unfortunately substantial amount of time), keeping proper ledgers for your operating account and multiple attorney trust accounts, performing the legal research and writing needed for each case, and actively double-checking to be sure you are following all of the professional rules of conduct. That list badly oversimplifies everything that goes into a solo law practice, but you get the point. Working for yourself means doing all the work yourself.

The crippling nature of comparison

With the benefit of hindsight, I can tell you that some of the behaviors I exhibited displayed a lack of confidence in myself and in what I offered. I fell prey to the crippling nature of comparison. When you compare yourself to someone else, you will almost inevitably find yourself comparing their strengths and the things you like about them to your own weaknesses and the things you dislike about yourself. By its very nature, comparing yourself to others will tear away at your self-esteem.

I struggled to believe in myself despite wonderful reviews from my clients. As a new lawyer running my own practice, I was desperately afraid of making mistakes. I was concerned about my age, and my level of experience, in an area where I was surrounded by senior lawyers. I knew I was smart enough to do the job, and do it well, even if I had to strategically ask for help with certain tasks. And yet, even knowing those things, I was unable to shake the feeling that because I was such a new lawyer and because I was less experienced than my competitors, I might not be good enough to have my own practice. I worked hard, but the results I needed were not materializing in the way I envisioned them, and that felt like evidence that I was not up to the task. I knew so many lawyers who were doing well working for other people. I compared what they were doing and what they were getting for it to my own, doubt-filled assessment of my solo practice, and I started to second-guess whether I truly had something good going on. All of the comparing I was doing was crippling my will and my ability to continue working for myself.

Charging less out of fear is a sign of low esteem

One of the ways you can tell that you need to boost your self-confidence is to notice when you are not properly taking care of your business. In particular, when you are afraid to charge people for the work that you do, or fail to properly protect yourself through contracts, you either have a lack of confidence in yourself or in the product or service that you are offering. The first point is straightforward: under-charging for your work is under-valuing yourself and what you can do. The second point is similar. When you fail to properly enter into a contract with someone, this shows that you do not value your product or service enough to protect it. Any savvy professional knows not to start work absent a contract; in a legal context, that means not starting work without your retainer paid, unless you have another fee arrangement that takes into account the risk you are taking by bringing on a client who is not paying you up front.

With all that said, here are some ways that you can boost your confidence in yourself and your business.

Education

If you are more educated than other people in your field in relation to a specific subject, highlight your education. For instance, there are many people who claim to be business consultants but who lack any education in business. I can take advantage of that: one way I am able to set myself apart from others is to highlight that I have a business-relevant education. Not only do I have a law degree, I also taught business law to paralegals at a local community college. Very few would-be consultants can say that they actually taught college students about business, and this makes me stand out.

If you do not have the education to give you this kind of credibility, right now is always a wonderful time to start getting it. Not all education has to be formal. A lot of what you learn in business will be through experience. Nonetheless, there are some important things you will need to know and be familiar with. Read. Read a lot. Whatever it is that you want to be doing, read and digest as much as you can about the field, the skills you might need, relevant tips and tricks, ways to get started, and so on. If you can find someone to mentor you on the subject matter, that makes a huge difference as well. Mentors can be powerful and effective ways to gain experience and become educated in a very specific area of business.

Uniqueness

We often overlook the things that make us inherently different from others. From early on, we are taught to fit in with everyone else. In most school systems, children are not taught to be independent thinkers. Whatever it is that you love to do, that you are passionate about, or that you are just really good at (and that maybe others are not so good at), highlight it! Connect the skills, abilities, choices, quirks, and talents that make you unique in some way to your business. Be creative, think outside of the box.

Clear vision

Have a clear vision of what you want your business to look like and where you want it to go. Once you have that vision, break it down into steps that you can take to make it happen. As you begin to accomplish those steps, you will find that your confidence will continue to grow. Not only that, but you will begin to dream bigger and begin to take more risks.

Taking more risks

Having confidence is almost a pre-requisite to taking risks. Most people have to feel that the risk they are taking is going to pay off; they need it not to feel risky. They have to feel that whatever they are doing is going to help them more than it hurts, frustrated, or exhausts them. As a calculated risk-taker myself, I have had challenges with taking risks. However, my experience has been that taking risks can sometimes be done with little to no confidence at all. This is not business-specific, and has everything to do with everyday life and how fear works. The risks we fail to take are usually complicated by some specific fear. Sometimes you confront a fear of rejection, a fear of losing money, or a fear of failing, and that prevents you from taking the leap that you need to. Whatever is holding you back from making bold choices is always the fear of something. Each time you practice overcoming that fear, your confidence will grow, freeing you to make bigger, bolder choices to support your growing business.

Facing your fears to boost your confidence

This part of the chapter expands on the theme of building your confidence. The biggest and most crucial part of that is learning to take risks, and taking risks requires facing your fears. You should do this one step at a time. Start with something manageable, and move up from there. To give you a sense of how this works, and how it will help you, I will draw on my own story again.

In the summer of 2014, I did something that I had never done before. I was at a place in my life where I felt stuck, and I desperately needed to break some of the cycles of fear I was living with. I was fortunate enough to realize that explicitly, and so I decided to deliberately and intentionally face a fear.

The fear I chose was to travel internationally, all by myself. I had never done such a thing, but what did I have to lose? Of course, my family and friends thought I "lost it," but I knew I needed to do something in order to move forward in my life. I knew, as they did not, that I was badly stuck. I was then, and still am, a fairly careful person, so it can sometimes take a lot for me to step out of my comfort zone. However, I have now grown to a place where I understand the importance of being out of my comfort zone and facing fears, and that growth very clearly began when I took my first solo international trip.

I traveled to Quetzaltenango, Xela, Guatemala. It was one of the most enriching experiences of my life. I stayed there for three weeks and studied Spanish language at an immersion school. I learned about Mayan culture, ate Guatemalan foods, stayed with a Guatemalan family, and loved every moment of it. I even met some people with whom I remain friends to this day.

And this is where my fear-facing started to really pay off, as my initial choice to take the trip began making it easier to face other fears as well. One of the friends I made convinced me to go cliff diving while I was there. I have always been afraid of heights, so this is not something I could have considered at any earlier time in my life. Coming from a woman who feared roller coasters, cliff diving was almost too much to take. But I was in the middle of successfully, joyfully living out an experience I had been scared of for years, and the support I took from that got me—literally—over the edge.

After I did the dive, I posted a photo and a video of the event on social media. Everyone was surprised that I had done something so risky, and so seemingly out of character. One of my followers asked me whether I was going to go skydiving next. I gave an unequivocal "no." In that moment, skydiving felt like insanity. But then, the reality of what I had just done started to sink in. Cliff diving was also a scary, almost unthinkable experience, but after I did it, I was glad that I had. And the same thing goes for having gone to Guatemala in the first place. Scary, but worth it.

That trip boosted my confidence. I came away from it feeling that if I could travel the world by myself, if I could cliff dive and survive, what did I really need to be afraid of? The positive experience of facing fears and being rewarded gave me the courage to take more risks in my personal life, and in my career.

Fast forward to two years later, and I did in fact jump out of a plane. In July of 2016, I went skydiving. Not indoor skydiving, but real-life skydiving. I found myself driving up to a small hangar in Baltimore County, Maryland, with a group of three friends from church. I questioned myself every second of the way. We had to wait an hour before the time came for us to board the small aircraft that would take us up. As it turned out, that was plenty of time to see several people ahead of us make the same jump. None of this helped absolve my jitters. When it was finally my turn, as we walked toward the plane, my dive instructor decided to take a video of me, asking me how I felt. "Nervous." I felt nervous, but I assured him that I prayed, and that we should be okay.

As the plane took off, I began to shiver, both because it was 20 degrees colder at 12,000 feet than it was on the ground, and because I was so nervous. The next thing I knew, the plane had reached the proper altitude, the doors flew open, and it was time to jump. My friend jumped first, with me and my instructor next in line. I did my best to enjoy the experience, because I had no intention of ever repeating it.

My instructor eased us closer and closer to the edge where the floor dropped off into sky. We sat on the edge and our legs dangled outside the aircraft. My instructor then used his hand to place the back of my head onto his should. He asked me if I was ready, I nodded, and we fell out of the plane. My "dive" was less of a "dive" than it was a "roll," but nonetheless we were airborne, and there I was, falling to the ground. The air blowing past was so strong that I could not open my mouth, and my checks were blown backwards. Five seconds into the dive, the instructor tapped my shoulders and instructed me to open my arms. There I was, flying. It was the most freeing thing I have ever felt. I looked around from side to side and saw the earth from a view I have never imagined. In that moment, I felt no fear.

Once we hit the ground, I understood what it meant to have an adrenaline high. I had never experienced such a euphoric feeling in my life. I felt invincible. I felt that if I could sky dive, there was nothing I could not do!

That is the positive cycle of risk-taking and fear-facing. The more fears you face, the more risks you will be able to take. The greater the risks you take, the more you can live your life in freedom from fear. This applies to business as much as it does to travel and having a fear of heights. The fewer fears you have, the more confidence you have, and the more risks you will take.

I get it. There are so many businesses out there! There are so many people doing the very thing that you want to do. And so many of them have more resources, more education, and more exposure than you do. But that should not stop you. It cannot stop you. If anything, it should spur you to figure out how you are different, and how you can use that difference to your advantage. Maybe you have a specific skillset due to your education. Maybe you have life experience doing something that they never have. Maybe you have a creative side to you that you can incorporate into your work to set you apart. Maybe the demographic or target audience that you go for is slightly different than that of your potential competitors; if so, make your products and advertising a little different to cater to that audience. There are so many ways you can diversify your message and your brand, all waiting right within you.

Reflect and Write

What is something you succeeded at that you did not feel you were good enough to do?

Have fears do you experience when it comes to starting your business?

What are some people you know of who succeeded when others did not think that they would?

Provide some examples of ideas that people laughed at, but that are doing well.

Chapter 4. Inner Work

The key to consistent forward movement, in
business and in life, is to focus your energy and
build toward what you want, and quit focusing on
what you do not want.

Have you ever tried to boost your own confidence and found that no

matter what you tried, it was not enough? Sometimes, despite all the

techniques for fear-facing and risk-taking, you find yourself in too low a

place, and it is difficult to climb out on your own. I have found myself in

just such a place, both in business and in life. And I have found that the

things that you tell yourself and believe about yourself make a huge

difference. The key to consistent forward movement is to focus your

energy, build toward exactly what you want, and quit expending effort on

what you do not want. *Protect your energy.*

In this chapter, I will share the story of one of the hardest moments

in my life: being KICKED OUT of law school. I will tell you how the effects of that moment were longstanding, and how the decision I made to protect my energy through it all changed the trajectory of my life and, ultimately, of my business.

The greatest lesson I learned from that situation is one you can apply to your own life. It is easy to believe that you are not good enough, once struggles and challenges drain the life out of you, and when the consequences of things completely beyond your control seem to be unending. Our low moments, mine and yours, are full of negative reinforcement; in the middle of my low point, I did not have enough strength within me to fend it off. And to top everything off, I was in a toxic relationship at that time, which was actively reinforcing some of those negative thoughts about myself. School, work, and life were just one big cycle that I could not seem to remove myself from. Though I worked hard on the outside to break that cycle by progressively improving my financial situation, the work I had to do inwardly to change my negative thoughts and destructive beliefs was far from over.

If a thought or belief is not productive, learn how to dismiss it. Learn how to take constructive criticism as helpful guidance, and be careful not to internalize harsh words. What you believe and say about yourself will determine how far you go. *Moguls* are amazingly good at this, almost to a fault. Many of them are accused of being arrogant, or even using sarcasm as a way to deflect the negative energy people try to weigh them down with.

Life-defining moments show us who we believe we are

In my personal journey, one majorly low and life-defining moment came at the beginning of law school, when I was kicked out after my first year. I was forced to petition a panel of professors and administrators at the school to let me back in. It was one of the most humbling, embarrassing, and heartbreaking moments of my life. It did not break my spirit, but something in me changed after it happened. The light inside me that once had been shining strong began to flicker. I was less sure of myself than I had ever been. I thought negative words to myself that I had never spoken aloud, but which echoed through and affected my entire life.

Watch your words, your heart is listening

> "If you don't have anything nice to say, then don't say it at all."

After having full-on fights with my siblings when I was a kid, my mother would always say, "If you don't have anything nice to say, then don't say it at all." It was a difficult expression for me to grasp at such a young age. As an adult, though, I realized that it applies to life in general, not just to that single situation. Our words have power, and as a consequence it is very important for us to watch what comes out of our mouths. One of the most important lessons from my journey is that as my thoughts and mindset became more positive, and as my words became more positive, my life began to change in a drastic and positive way.

Nowhere has this been more true than during my legal education. As a law student, it seemed there was always a challenge that I had to overcome. The first semester of law school was especially tough for me. It was my first time being away from home and from my support system. I was in an entirely new state, where I had to make new friends and adjust to a new way of life. This was made harder by the fact that when I was not in class, most of my time was spent studying. There was not much to do in the area where I lived, so I did not leave the house much. The law school was located in a very rural area, and I lived right up the street from the campus, practically within walking distance. There was a cornfield in my back yard and cotton fields directly up the street. It was common to drive pass a herd of cattle, and to be on roads without street lights. In other words, the environment required a huge adjustment from the suburban life I was accustomed to. That adjustment took effort, which was reflected in my grades.

At the law school I attended, students had to maintain a cumulative average of 76% at the end of each year in order to stay in school. My grades at the end of the first semester, with all its difficult adjustments and settling-in, left me with a running average of 73%. That meant that I had to have at least a 78.113% average on my final exams in the second semester, in order to bring my cumulative average to at least a 76%. Yes, that is a frustratingly random number, but it was based on the amount of credit hours I was taking each semester. If I did not raise my grade point average to that 78.113%, I would risk losing my scholarship and possibly being "excluded," or kicked out of school.

It happened, I was kicked out of law school

> "The problem is not your writing, but maybe you
> should consider another career." (My professor.)

My school claimed that the grading of our final exams was anonymous, but what happened to me at the end of my second semester left me questioning the truth of that.

I am going to spend some extra time giving you the details of how I was kicked out of school. I want to ensure that you know something about the environment where this took place, and I want to share what happened well enough that you can understand why this experience was so life-defining for me. If all goes well, by the end of the chapter, you will be ready to trace the parallels between my life and your own.

As we have established, all of this took place at the end of my second semester of law school. Those critical final exams had ended, the tests were graded, and I had the opportunity to review my results. I had two classes in my first year that were taught by the same professor, one in each semester. The first semester, I was ranked 90th out of 127 students in the first-year class. The second semester, I was ranked 28th out of 127. The same professor taught both classes, and I was sure that my extreme improvement meant that my final exam would be full of nice comments and check marks. I was wrong.

I read through the entire exam to see what I got right and what I got wrong. On the very last page, the professor left their general comments. One of these—the only one that mattered, I feel—read that I "did not have a problem with writing," but that "I should consider another career." This professor was telling me that I should not continue on to become a lawyer. This professor, teacher of the very same class in which I had just outscored 78% of the entire first-year population, was telling me to quit. I could not believe it. It did not make any sense to me. And most of all, if the grading was anonymous, why was such a targeted comment left on my exam?

I left the classroom that day feeling deflated. I spoke to a professor I trusted about what had happened, and he reasoned that the professor in question might just have been trying to motivate me. He said that the other professor was old-school, and stuck in his ways. That maybe he was just using some sort of cruel reverse psychology to help me continue doing well. I was not convinced. It felt unkind and aggressive.

Even through it all, it never crossed my mind to quit, not even when I was kicked out. That second semester, I had done everything in my power to ensure that my grades would improve, so that I could keep my scholarship and stay in school, but things did not work out that way. After I reviewed my exam scores, I saw my average grade for the whole year: 75.64%. Only 0.36 away from 76%. I missed the required standard by 0.36%.

The school sent me a letter and told me that I would be kicked out of school. I remember feeling disbelief more than anything else. I was always such an overachiever, and was able to accomplish whatever I put my mind to—and then some! I cried, reading that letter, because even though I knew that I would not quit, it just felt so deeply wrong and *unfair* to be kicked out of school over such a small percentage. And there was more: in addition to being kicked out of school, I was notified that they would be taking my scholarship. The only reason I had attended that school in the first place was because I had been given a scholarship, so the whole situation now felt almost absurd. Still, I was determined not to quit. Two things kept me going. First, I was raised to finish what I started, and this situation was no different from any other in that regard. And second, I had entered law school confused about my career, and I did not know what else I could do with my degree, or how else to pay my school loans. So, both determined and without alternatives, I stuck with it.

In the school's letter, they outlined my options for appealing the decision. The letter told me that I had to submit a petition to the school in order to get back in. There were no other choices. If I did not take this opportunity, I would have to pack my things and go home.

Other students received the same letter, and many of them were my friends and study partners. At the beginning of law school, the students in each class were sectioned off into three groups. Each group attended their core classes together, and often studied together as well. The section you started with in your first year was the same section you would stick with for the rest of your law school career. These were important people in your life, all the more so because the city our school was in was only six miles across, so we did not have much to do other than study!

I learned that two other people from my study group faced the same situation I did, and were also petitioning to stay at school. More than that, five out of the only eleven people of color among the school's student population of three hundred—nine whom happened to be first year students, and none of whom were in the second year—were excluded from school as well. The other students of color were also friends of mine. We had all stuck together for the most part. In our attempts to be included and accepted by the rest of our classmates, we were often met with resistance or flat-out apathy. Most of us were not used to being in such a small town, and we found comfort and familiarity in one another's presence. Even though we were from different places, culture is culture. With so many of my closest friends and companions on their way out of the school, it would prove to be a very lonely road ahead.

The petition process was grueling. It required that I stay at school instead of going home over summer break, to try to beg my way back into this program. The process required that we write a letter petitioning for readmission and explaining why we should be let back in. Once we submitted the letter, they would give us a day and a time to arrive at the school for a hearing. We would then stand before a panel of professors and administrators who would decide whether we would be granted the opportunity to return.

When I walked into school on the day of the hearing, I found myself sitting around a long table alongside several people I had grown to love as friends and colleagues. The majority of us were people of color. I waited there as they called each person's name, and one by one they went into the room. I sat there for hours. The anxiety I felt was acute the whole time, and peaked every time the organizer came to the door and called another name. I felt my heart pounding, and my eyes swelling with tears each time they called a name that was not mine. It got later and later in the day, and my name was still not called. At the end of the day, I was the last person waiting at the table. They came in and gave me a piece of paper, informing me that my petition was accepted. I would not have to go before the panel, I would only have to meet certain academic conditions set by the school. I had to retake one class, and take another class during my final year rather than earlier on. And, of course, I had to keep my grades up.

I felt so much relief knowing that I would be able to continue. I was almost ready to move on and put the experience behind me, right up until I found out that I was the ONLY student admitted back into the program. Several others were told they could be readmitted if they repeated their first year, others were refused point-blank.

I would learn later that both my friends from study group were forced to repeat their first year of law school. I had to find new study groups willing to let me join them, and go to most of my classes as the only person of color. Having graduated from George Washington University in the District of Columbia, it was not new for me to be the only person of color in a classroom, but this felt different. I was much farther away from home, farther outside my comfort zone, and cut off from my support system. I simply was not prepared to be hundreds of miles away from home, facing a situation like that alone.

I was fortunate. I was able to connect with other classmates and start a new study group, and dive back into my work. I felt guilty and blessed at the same time. I had been very close with some of those students who were excluded, and some of those made to repeat their first years. As I worked to make new friends and acquaintances, I was walking a lonely, difficult road. I could not understand why I had been chosen to continue on, while the others had not. It might have been that I was so close to the cut-off grade percentage, having missed it by only 0.36%, but some of the other students were extremely close to the cut-off as well. There was no logic to the process that any of us could find.

But, finally, with the ordeal over, I went back home to spend the rest of the summer with my family.

Do not let labels become who you are

I headed back to my home state, joyful and relieved. In the moment, I lacked the perspective to realize that the words my professor wrote on my exam had settled themselves deep inside me, and that they doubt they created would influence how I felt about myself for the rest of my law school career, and into my legal career thereafter. In the short-term, things felt okay. When I returned home, I was welcomed with all the love and support that I so desperately needed. Initially, I slept for about a solid week, as the emotional exhaustion of the recent ordeal caught up with me. I soaked up as much family and friend time as I possibly could before summer ended. I remember feeling a terrifying pit forming in my stomach when it was time to go back. I remember crying as I left home for the five-hour drive back to school. And I remember knowing that I had to finish this part of my journey, no matter how hard it was.

Let your failures focus and motivate you

I remember what it felt like, knowing that everyone knew what happened. Information about exclusions and hearings was supposed to be anonymous, but word got around nonetheless. I felt even more strongly that I did not belong in that environment, but I also felt that I had to prove myself. Prove that I belonged there, prove it to myself, to my professors, to my peers. I also felt I had to demonstrate that I was just as smart as my classmates, that I could do whatever they could. I am not sure, on the whole, whether this was a good or a bad thing, but it did motivate me to work even harder at my studies. I am a competitive person by nature, and what I went through forced me to compete with myself, not with anyone else. I had no time to focus on what everyone else was doing. And this paid off, although, as I will talk about shortly, all the stress and focusing came with its own set of issues.

When adversity narrows your options, get creative

Because the school placed additional requirements on my law school journey, I was prevented from following many of the standard career paths most law students followed. As a result of what happened during my first year, I had to retake two of my courses, and they also mandated which courses I would take in my third year. As a result, I spent most of my second year making sure I kept all of my scores up, whereas other students were seeking out internships and studying abroad.

It is standard practice for law-school students to begin applying for jobs during their second year of school. Law firms typically begin recruiting entry-level lawyers for associate positions through their summer programs. By accepting you as an intern or extern for a summer, they gave themselves an opportunity to gauge your work, and as a result they would often hire you full-time once you graduated. Due to my academic situation, I opted not to seek one of those summer positions, and instead took summer courses to ensure that I stayed up to par in class. I also wanted to be certain that I would graduate on time, because I did not want to take on any additional student loans. So, I found a summer study program in Washington, D.C., and did an externship with one of my professors to earn additional credit. I completed both, and headed back to North Carolina for my third year of law school. As you can see, the entire situation—being kicked out, petitioning for readmission, and the resulting requirements—effectively shaped how the rest of my law school career would develop.

My third year of law school was spent studying and applying for judicial clerkships and other junior positions. My hope was to be employed by graduation. Unfortunately, I landed interviews but no positions. I was hindered in part by the large-print notice of my having been excluded that was displayed so prominently on my transcript. The pain and destruction from that first-year event would follow me for years. On the inside, I knew that I was not a reflection of that school year, but my profession was unable to see otherwise. Being kicked out of school had disqualified me from many of the jobs I applied for, and had discouraged me from applying to many more. I started to think that a legal career would never happen for me, and that maybe, I was just not good enough.

I ended up deferring most of my student loans until I found a position that would enable me to pay them. Student loan debt became another burden, another weight I carried from law school, and another reason for me to feel like I was not good enough to succeed.

I escaped these weights only by, eventually, deciding that I would not let someone else's approval or denial of my job applications determine my destiny. I started my own practice. I worked long, and I worked hard. I used my spare time to develop more business concepts, which I am now putting into practice through my new business. The lesson here is that everything you go through can, and will, work in your favor if you use your focus to learn from it and build on whatever it leads you to.

Doing your inner work

I eventually made the decision to change my life, after facing so many obstacles, time and again. What I mean by that is this: I decided to take inventory of what I was feeling, of what I was saying to myself, and of why I believed that my life was going in the direction it was. I used that information deliberately and intentionally to change the things I could, and change my perspective on things I could not. I took stock, and I did my outer and inner work.

Inner work is not something that happens overnight. For me, it was a lengthy process. (Some of the techniques and supports I relied on during this period will be discussed in more detail in Chapter 10, Take Care of Yourself.) I relied heavily on prayer, meditation, social support and time with loved ones, volunteering my time to charity, positive affirmations, exercise, and setting boundaries with my time and against negative people. These are all good options during difficult times, because they cause you to focus on yourself in a healthy way. And in addition to focusing on yourself and building yourself up, they cause you to use your energy to help others. When we are focused on what we love, on what we do well, and on helping others, we naturally begin to heal and move forward as the negativity and the things holding us back are lessened.

Who we allow around us, what we allow them to say to us, and what we ultimately choose to believe about them and ourselves will affect our energy. At the end of the day, we get to choose whether that will be in a positive or a negative way. I began to be more careful about who and what was around me, and began to adjust my patterns and actions based on how the relationships around me felt. As I began to rid my life of the more negative relationships, things began to drastically shift for me, in a positive direction. (I have more to say about the importance of your circle and your social network in Chapter 9.)

My life has changed tremendously over the last three years. The trick, ultimately, was to quit focusing what I did not want, and to build toward those parts of the future that I knew I wanted.

Reflect and Write

What are some negative things that people have said about you or told you that you believe?

What are the tragedies in your life that you've held on to and that have hindered your progress?

What are the negative things you say to yourself?

What are some positive things you can say to yourself to counteract those negative thoughts and beliefs?

What are some positive affirmations you can say to yourself every day?

What are some ways you can change your life today to move in a more positive direction?

How can you quit focusing on the old and use your energy to build the new?

Chapter 5. Persist and Persevere

They have honed the ability to know their limits
and to persevere only when it is healthy to.

Persist and persevere for yourself

Entrepreneurship is hard.

Many of the most successful entrepreneurs you see, *moguls*, have also

persevered through tremendous adversity. Some have endured

homelessness, bankruptcies, unbelievable pressures, multiple failed

business ventures, rejections, harsh criticisms, and more. What separates

them from unsuccessful entrepreneurs is that they did not give up when

they encountered these obstacles. They have honed the ability and the determination to persevere and persist. They have also honed their sense of their own limits, allowing them to persevere only when it is healthy to do so.

One of the primary examples of perseverance in my life was making it through law school and passing the bar exam on my first attempt. You have already read that story, and know about the obstacles I had to overcome, first in order to graduate and then, ultimately, to become a licensed attorney. In no way was it easy, but it certainly prepared me for the challenges and struggles through which I would have to persevere as I started my businesses, and it helped me to set personal limits for what I would choose to endure.

As I look back on my journey through entrepreneurship, one of the things that I find myself wondering is where my solo practice would be by now, if I had been able to stick with it. There were times when I had more clients than I needed, and times when clients did not pay or were not paying on time. Other times, there were no calls and no money coming through the door at all! There was no way to tell which of those situations I would find myself in during any given month. I was fortunate enough that I was able to save money on good months to help take care of the bills on slower months, but even so the uncertainty of my finances placed a serious strain on my ability to rest, and, ultimately, on my health. I was constantly stressed about paying my bills; I watched my student loans capitalizing in the background, doubling and even tripling in size, and knowing that I had to start paying the interest on them soon as I could. I had two choices: I could start bringing in consistent, paying clientele who would ensure my bills and loan interest would be paid, or I could get a full-time job working for someone else, taking care of my immediate financial needs while I built the firm on a part-time basis.

Because I was not able to predict whether clients would appear consistently and pay consistently, I chose option two and started applying for jobs. Ultimately, I started work as a contract attorney for large firms.

Sometimes, I look back and wonder what my life would look like if I had made a different decision. What if, instead of finding a job working for someone else, I powered through those tough financial moments, letting my loans grow even more and enduring lean months? Yes, I felt I was making the best decision I could at the time, even though it meant working for myself only part-time, but what did I sacrifice by doing so?

There's no way to tell. I know other attorneys, who started their law practices at the same time I did and kept going with them, whose firms are now doing well. However, I do my best not to compare myself to others because everyone's situation is different (as we discussed in Chapter 4). Some of those lawyers were not burdened by student loans, others had help or resources that could assist them with their business hardships. I did not. I persevered for as long as my person situation allowed me to.

This lesson is extremely important. You need to know what you can handle, and when you need to preserve yourself mentally, physically, spiritually, and emotionally. This kind of preservation is the other side of persistence; both are necessary. For me, the stress of my financial situation became sustainable for me in the long term. I knew that, under those conditions, preserving my mental health was more important than persisting with the business. I also knew that someday I would be able to go back and try again. I was not sure that I would, but the option was there if I wanted to take it.

When I decided to work for myself, I was taking on a special kind of burden. A burden accepted out of necessity and established through creativity, in order to be able to live. This was not the burden of having job requirements to meet, it was the burden of being responsible for my own success. It required overcoming many challenges I would otherwise have been able to avoid. I have spoken about how difficult it was to increase my clientele in the middle of a very saturated market for attorneys. I have spoken about the uncertainty and inconsistency of my income as a result. I had to quickly become competent in areas of law I had never practiced, and all of this was just so that I could stay afloat. There are many other parts to this story to this, but that first year is enough to get the core message across: persist, persevere, and preserve.

When other people say no, do not let that be the end for you

Working for yourself means that you will have to handle lots of people. You will have to deal with clients, investors, suppliers, support staff, and many others. There will be situations where you will have to pitch a product or sell yourself. There will be situations where you will need additional financing. At some point along your journey, you will be told "no." And you will likely hear that "no" more loudly than you hear the many "yes" answers that came first. Get used to it. You are going to face more rejection that you could ever imagine as you start your own business. Some or all of that rejection will come from the very people who you think are going to support you in what you are doing and where you want to go. Rejection is just a part of business. You are going to be in positions where you pitch your idea, your book, your movie, your product, or your service and no one responds. Or, if they do respond, all they give you is a "no." Do not let your fear of rejection or your fear of hearing "no" stop you from persevering in entrepreneurship.

When "no" means "keep trying"

More often than not, when you are running a business, being told "no" means you need to "keep trying." *Moguls* know better than to quit after being told "no." I remember when I first decided to open my law practice, with no money available and minimal resources. As a new graduate, I had nothing saved and had to figure things out quickly. When I opened my operating account for the new business, I went to the bank alongside a friend, because he was doing the same for his business. They asked him if he wanted to apply for a business line of credit with the bank, which he would be able to use for his business in short-term, and in the long-term, would allow him to open a business credit card account and apply for a business loan. He applied, and was approved.

It was my turn. I sat down at the desk and submitted all the proper paperwork to the customer service representative. They asked me the same questions they had him, and I decided that I, too, would apply for a business line of credit through the bank. My application was denied, on the grounds that I did not have a source of income. And yet, how was I supposed to have income before getting the business up and running? My intention had been to use the line of credit for exactly that—to get me started, and to help establish my income.

I did not let that "no" stop me. Instead, it meant that I had to get creative. Lacking an office, I used virtual office spaces or public spaces (coffee shops and libraries) to meet clients in. Office supplies and equipment came from all over. One of my cousins was giving away a used computer; she knew I was starting a business and asked me if I wanted it. When I say "used," I am being kind—the computer was at least seven years old. But I accepted her offer, and she got the system ready for me to use. I used my old printer from law school, and my home internet connection. I bought my desk and two filing cabinets from a yard sale. A local church had closed the school it had been running and was selling all of its furniture. It was all old, wooden, and bulky, but it served its purpose. I now had a computer, printer, internet, desk, and two filing cabinets.

These things got me through my first year of full-time entrepreneurship and several years of part-time practice. I still have the filing cabinets, and they are still in great condition.

That story is just one example of how you cannot let rejection stop you. If I let the bank's rejection stop me from starting my business, I would not have the experience, background, and confidence to be writing this book; I never would have become an entrepreneur.

Some of what you will have to persevere through will involve emotional obstacles as well as physical obstacles ones. Overcoming these obstacles requires the kind of "inner work" that we discussed in Chapter 4. Entrepreneurship is a perpetual cycle of overcoming obstacles; these are often financial, but can also be very emotional. If you are experiencing an emotional obstacle as part of your entrepreneurship journey, please be mindful and practice self-care. I will address this more thoroughly in Chapter 10.

I will give just one example of an emotional obstacle here. Before I started my firm, I anticipated that after being in business for a year, I would have made it to a place of "success." At that time, I defined success as having a steady income that allowed me to pay myself, pay my bills, and grow my company. Boy, was I wrong. After one year, I felt that I had barely gotten any closer to where I wanted to be. That frustrated me, and made it hard to see any value in continuing to work for myself. That is a classic emotional obstacle that you will very likely face.

Of the lawyers I know who became "successful" in private practice, most of them took at least three years in business to do so—years they spent stressed, worried, and facing financial and emotional challenges. Before starting my own business, I had heard that most companies have already either died off or succeeded by their third year, but I had assumed that I would be able to beat the odds at least through year one. No one warned me of how difficult it would be to struggle for so long, and with so much uncertainty. This leads me to a discussion of overnight successes.

Overnight success takes ten years of work

No, I do not have any research or hard numbers to back up my statement that overnight success takes ten years. However, I have noticed a pattern. Many of companies that are successful and have great visibility needed ten or more years to get where they are. Whether the business itself was cultivated for ten years, or the owners had been cultivating their skillsets for that amount of time, ten seems to be the magic number.

The question then is, what does that mean for us? It means that we have no excuse. If we really want "success," we have to bear the ups and downs of entrepreneurship. Remember the perpetual cycle of overcoming obstacles I spoke about a moment ago? *Moguls* know how to persist and persevere through them all.

I am going to take a brief detour here to highlight some companies that illustrate this point well. First: the founder of Pandora was turned down for financing more than 300 times. When you think about how most people tend to behave, they do not find it too difficult to keep going after just one rejection. You might think that it was just a bit of bad luck. After the fifth time, most people would start to rethink what they were doing, and maybe start second-guessing themselves. This man endured "no" for *hundreds* of times, and, no matter how that made him feel, he did not waver in his pursuit. Talk about persistence and perseverance!

A second example is Apple. Apple was founded in 1976 and did not become a household name for almost a decade, when it released the Macintosh personal computer in 1984. Prior to that year, Apple sold computers almost exclusively for to businesses, and most people did not have computers in their homes. It took the company eight years to create a product that would change technological history and, ultimately, the history of the United States. Their failed attempts included the Apple III and Apple Lisa, both large projects. What if Apple had quit after those failures? They would never have created the Macintosh, the world of technology would be a very different place, and it would have taken us much longer to have personal computers in our homes. Apple may have been an overnight success, but they took years of struggling to get there.

Are you afraid of criticism?

> "Sticks and stones may break my bones but words
> will never hurt me."

Or so we all think, right up until we put our blood, sweat, and tears into building our business, only to then have someone say unkind things about it. In a day and age where technology can be used as a tool to build your business and credibility, technology can also, just as quickly, bring them down. I have seen, countless times now, how bad reviews or negative comments on social media can tank an otherwise successful small company. Insults and bad reviews are very different, however, from constructive criticism. Constructive criticism can be some of the most valuable feedback you can receive. If it is true and offers good suggestions, your company is best served by listening to the advice and making positive adjustments. When companies do not respond to constructive criticism in this way, they risk being capsized by the very thing they refused to accept and acknowledge.

> Criticism can be helpful; insults can tell you what other people are insecure about.

An example of constructive criticism is when someone who has turned down your product or pitch is still willing to give you advice or information about what you could do to improve it. Another example is when someone on your team offers their candid advice on why, and in what way, something is not going to work, and suggests another way of doing it. Remember also that sometimes constructive criticism is not offered in a way that shows you how to improve. Sometimes someone will just tell you that something is a bad idea or does not work well, and that feedback may not be coming from a bad place. When this happens, you have to make a judgement call as to whether there is any truth to what they are saying.

And then, of course, there are time when someone is just insulting you. Most of us know when we are being insulted. Review the information people offer you, make the best judgment calls you can, and adjust your process if need be. If you are especially creative, you can even use some of the most negative things that are said about you to your advantage.

Adapting through changing circumstances

Another way you can persist and persevere is by adapting your ideas and goals to match changing circumstances. As you go through your entrepreneurship journey, you will learn that the only thing that stays constant is the presence of change. You will have to change plans, shift focus, and often compromise on things you did not plan to. You will have to find new solutions to problems. Entrepreneurship will be one of the most unpredictable challenges you have ever taken on. Even with the best business plan, teams, board of directors, boards of trustees, and fundraisers, there will always be curve balls thrown at you. If you are not adaptable, you should probably learn to be.

In addition to being adaptable, though, you can also cut down the number of curve balls coming your way. Try consulting with more than one knowledgeable person about your idea (protecting it, of course, using a non-disclosure agreement) so that people with different perspectives can help you identify blind spots in your plans or thought processes.

Re-inventing yourself as a way to adapt

Re-inventing yourself is just as important in business as it is in everyday life. If you have a plan that is not working well, be willing to go back to the drawing board and start over. At the very least, be willing to modify what you have to make it better. The most successful companies understand what it means to re-invent themselves, and do so as often as necessary. Others die off thanks to their unwillingness to change. Blockbuster is an example of a company that failed to re-invent itself to match changing times; Redbox and Netflix came onto the market and Blockbuster was no longer a viable option for consumers. Blockbuster failed to utilize technology in a world that increasingly relied on it, much to their detriment.

Adaptability in your personal life

Your perseverance in entrepreneurship depends on whether you tend to persevere through challenges in your personal life. The tendency to persevere applies to every area of life, and in your relationships as well.

Your ability to adapt to changes and curve balls is something that says a lot about who you are.

Part of what this means is that you can practice adaptability in your private life in order to be more successful as an entrepreneur. Both the attitude and the habits of perseverance can be cultivated through time and experience. It is not easy to continue with a project, a dream, or a plan after you have failed or been denied. It is not easy to keep asking when you're told "no" time and time again. It is not easy to adapt when things do not go as you envisioned them. But now that you understand that perseverance is a major part of what it takes to succeed at entrepreneurship, you can make decisions that reflect that priority. Again, entrepreneurship is not for everyone. Some of you may weigh the pros and cons, and decide that the cost of entrepreneurship is not worth the effort. I have been there myself, and sometimes it is just one stage if the growth process, and all you need it to take a breather and start again when you are ready. Only you know yourself well enough to tell.

Reflect and Write

What are some times in your life or business when you have given up? How could you have handled the situation differently? What have you learned from it?

What are you going to do to plan for hardship in your business?

What is an affirmation you can offer yourself the next time you are rejected in the course of building your business?

What are some examples of entrepreneurs you look up to who persevered through their own struggled?

What are some things they did to keep going?

How can you be more creative in your current business to let you overcome obstacles more easily?

Chapter 6. Be Bold and Relentless

In order to truly master entrepreneurship, you are
going to have to push your boundaries and always
aim higher!

Take a moment and think about some of the greatest entrepreneurs you

know of, or have seen, and bring to mind their levels of boldness and

confidence. As we learned in a previous chapter, *moguls* are no strangers

to adversity. They know how to persist and persevere over and over

again. They know how to keep going after they have been told "no"

many times, after their ideas have failed to work thousands of times, after

they saw no returns on their investments despite hundreds of asks.

Moguls are relentless at the pursuit of doing whatever is needed to ensure

that their business succeeds.

I made a big, bold move when I opened my own law practice in

2012. I opened a business as a leap of faith rather than a calculated

development choice. Once I opened the practice, I then had to be relentless in doing everything I could to get the exposure I needed to draw in clientele. Not only did I write for newspapers, teach courses to the community, and sign up for services where I could receive referrals, I also had my own blog and website. Every day I was writing at least three articles: one for my blog, one for local newspapers, and one for online publishers looking for legal content. That adds up to a lot of work, when combined with everything else I had to do for the firm. Sometimes it felt like I was doing far too much! Yet, I persisted until I no longer could.

This chapter builds on Chapter 5; persistence and perseverance are characteristics you see in people who are bold and relentless. What I understand about entrepreneurship now, but did not understand back then, is that it can be okay to change what you are doing. It is okay to rebrand. It is okay to make changes and adjustments based on what you need and the direction you see your business going in. It is okay to evolve, and transform your work into something different than you envisioned it being. Guide your choices here based on what will allow you to be passionate about your work and make the best decisions for your business. I was under the impression that once I started my business based on one model, I had to stick with that plan, no matter what. To this day, people are still calling to ask me to take on family law contracts, even though I long ago ceased to practice in that area. I did not particularly enjoy family law, but I was fearful to let go of it because I knew it well, and it was my most reliable source of business. This contributed to my many burnouts, and ultimately, to my willingness to scale back my solo practice.

Moguls often go through many transformations before they find exactly where they want to be. And even when they get there, they have to continue to evolve in order to stay relevant and profitable as the market changes. *Moguls* are not afraid to change their brands; they are not afraid to offer new services or products that complement their identity.

As a brief detour from our narrative here, it is worth noting a few celebrities who represent this point especially well: "Prince" and "Diddy." In 1993, the artist "Prince" changed his name to an unpronounceable symbol, and was referred to for a while as "the artist formerly known as Prince." This gave him a new identity, and while many people did not understand it, the force of his brand was undeniable. Not only was it instantly recognizable, it was also unique and therefore interesting.

Moguls are not afraid even to change their identities and brands completely. For instance, consider Sean Combs, who now goes by

"Diddy." He also has been known "as Puff Daddy" and "P. Diddy." In addition to his musical career, he has found success in the clothing and alcohol industries, and currently has a whole vodka collection as part of his brand. Both music and alcohol products complement the hip-hop industry very well, because hip-hop glorifies clothing and alcohol-heavy partying. In other words, Diddy knows his audience.

Moguls are also open to constructive criticism, and are able to quickly readjust when they make business moves that turn out not to be in the best interests of their company. They are bold and relentless when it comes to succeeding at whatever they do.

Being bold means facing embarrassment

If you really want to be successful in entrepreneurship, you will have to grow your capacity for enduring embarrassment. *Moguls* are masters at taking business risks, and whenever you take risks, there is a possibility that you will find yourself in a situation that leaves you and your company open to criticism, attacks, or ridicule. And so, if you fear embarrassment, it is unlikely that you will make it far as an entrepreneur. At its root, the fear of embarrassment is a fear of rejection, and as I discussed in Chapter 5, rejection is an unavoidable part of the journey of being an entrepreneur.

Remember our discussion about believing in yourself and your product? Part of that is being bold in how you value your business. If you charge a certain fee, stick to it. Quit negotiating and lowering your prices for people. People will only believe that you are worth what you are bold enough to charge (so long as the price is also backed up by the quality of your service or product). Get used to asking for what you want and what you are worth without thinking twice. You will attract your target customers only when you stick to your guns. Remember, not everyone is going to be in your target market, and not everyone is looking for what you offer. Even among people who are, many may not be willing to pay the fee you charge. They will always have other options for finding the service or product they wanted from you, but that does not diminish the value of what you offer.

Even Goliath was not invincible

Have you ever felt afraid of how big your entrepreneurial dreams are? Have you ever been afraid of the competition? Then you are in excellent company. My point here is best made with a Biblical reference, to the story of David and Goliath. It can be found in book of 1 Samuel, chapter 17. The story illustrates how underdogs can find victory against overwhelming odds. Goliath was a giant, said to have been nine feet tall. David was just a shepherd boy, who found himself volunteering to fight Goliath when no one else was willing to. David arrived at the battlefield and saw his older brothers and the rest of the Israeli army cowering in fear of Goliath, the Philistine champion. He knew that someone had to step up and fight Goliath for his people to defend the land that belonged to them. David stepped up. He showed no fear. Unlike the other soldiers, David had no armor, and his weapon of choice was a humble slingshot. He chose five smooth stones and went to battle. David killed Goliath with the very first stone that he cast from his slingshot.

It can be so easy to look out at the competition, our very own Goliaths, and, fearful of challenging them, shy away from what we want to do in our hearts. In this age of social media, keeping track of our competition and what is around us is only natural, and may actually be good for you. In order to beat the competition, you need to study it, identify its weaknesses, and harness your strengths to exploit them. Treat your business's competitors and obstacles as your Goliath, and go boldly forward to overcome them.

Finding your niche

When I was in the early stages of building my second business, and my personal brand along with it, one of the problems I encountered was that there were too many people claiming to provide the same service I wanted to offer, many of them lacking the requisite education or experience. I was blown away by the sheer number of people whose bios and profile pages described them as business consultants and public speakers. Confronting this, I felt that maybe I did not want to be known as a business consultant, that I might need to change my brand or my goals. *Moguls* are great at identifying their specific niche, and branding themselves in ways that make them stand out within it. (When I say niche, I am speaking about an area of specialization and a target audience.)

The challenge for me was deciding how I wanted to brand myself, and how to do it in a way that would capture the fact that I am a business consultant and public speaker, without explicitly branding myself using only those terms, as neither would stand out on Instagram, Facebook, and other social media platforms. I settled on "business law" and "estate planning" as key phrases to distinguish myself from competitors, and have noticed a clear difference in my internet traffic and service as a result!

Let me be honest here. It is very difficult to create something truly new and innovative. If you are creating something yourself, it was likely inspired by someone else's previous work, which you are merely building on. Of course, there is absolutely nothing wrong with that! But it does present a challenge: how do you convince people that what you offer is better than the original product or service that you are building on? Customers make purchases based on the person selling the product, not just because of products themselves. There should be a market for what you are attempting to sell, but that alone is not enough if you cannot market your own brand, credibility, and image as the business owner.

In the very rare event that you are creating something totally innovative, it is important that you ask yourself lots of questions. These include: Is there a market for my product? How much money will it take for me to create it? How much money will it take for it to be manufactured and distributed? How much can I sell it for? Will it be profitable? Does it make the lives of my target market easier? Does it solve a problem? Do I have the resources needed to protect this idea by getting a trademark and/or patent?

As you work through these questions, something I call FOCO can start to come into play.

FOCO = Fear of Copying Ideas

Some people are afraid of being innovative and putting their new products out there for the world to see. Often this is due to the fear that someone will steal their ideas and replicate them. Some say that copying is the sincerest form of flattery; others say that it is just plain wrong. I fall somewhere in the middle. Regardless, if you have an idea or product that is truly innovative, and you have done all of the research and planning necessary to blaze that bold new trail, do not let FOCO stop you. Do not be afraid to take a leap of faith and launch that product or service. There are ways you can protect yourself and your new intellectual property, as well as non-disclosure agreements you can use while you are in the process of building the business. Be careful whom you share your ideas with, but do not pass up the opportunity all together. Make sure you are getting support from people who can help your vision come to fruition.

Some of the biggest obstacles, both perceived and real, can be overcome just by facing that fear instead of running from it. If you are intimidated by the size of the task, and you allow that to deter you from walking forward, you will never know what is on the other side of your fear. You will never complete your entrepreneurship journey. *Moguls* are masters at disciplining and training themselves to prepare for competition and obstacles. They approach them head-on rather than shying away. The next time you feel intimidated by competition or an obstacle in your path, remember that it can be overcome. Remember that Goliath can be slain. Remember that you are uniquely prepared to do exactly what you are doing. Strategize, focus, and handle everything that comes your way with boldness.

Some people are born with a natural boldness in them. There are also some people who are born with the spirit to persevere. Whether or not you have the natural inclination to be bold and relentless, one thing that will help you build that bold and unrelenting spirit is life experience. This leads us to our next crucial lesson.

Give yourself credit

Sometimes, we do not give ourselves enough credit. We have all had to overcome obstacles and challenges in our lives; you can probably think of some of those moments as you read this. When you overcome adversity, it gives you confidence that the next time you feel challenged, you will overcome it again. The same is true in business. If you exercise a bold and relentless attitude, even in the face of rejection, competition, and obstacles, eventually none of those will feel burdensome or intimidating as you move forward in your entrepreneurship journey. That also means that you will be able to freely take more risks and receive higher pay offs for doing so.

The rule of thumb here is simple: small risk, small return on investment; bigger risk, bigger return on investment. Boldness leads to greater willingness to take bigger risks, which ultimately lead to bigger payoffs.

Reflect and Write

What part of your business experience has caused you to cower in fear?

How can you face that fear head on?

What challenges have you overcome that you have overlooked?

Take a moment to think about the things you have overcome and write three things you are grateful for.

Chapter 7. Making and Managing Your Mistakes

You will make mistakes

This chapter is about making mistakes in your business, and how to manage your business properly in the wake of those mistakes. I am going to show you how you can proactively protect both yourself and your business when dealing with others, and how you can recover when things go wrong. At one point or another, you will be taken advantage of in the process of building your business. You are going to have money stolen from you. You are going to provide a service that you wish you had charged more for. You are going to enter into business relationships based on trust rather than using a contract, and regret it later. When you are first starting out in business, you will make a lot of mistakes, unless you have mentors who can guide you and a legal framework that can protect you properly.

Know when to break a deal

There have been several situations in my life in which I faced the choice of staying in, or walking away from, a difficult relationship. Some of the most difficult of these came during my entrepreneurship journey. The very first time I walked away from a business connection was when I decided to stop working as a full-time solo law practitioner back in 2013, after being my own boss for a whole year. The firm was doing reasonably well, and gaining momentum more and more quickly, but I badly needed steadier income and lower stress. When you are first starting out, entrepreneurship is just not very steady, and sticking it out was not an option for me at that time.

A more recent situation that I had to walk away from was a book project I joined up with in late 2017. My money was stolen from me, and I chose to cut my losses and abandon the project. What happened was roughly this: I saw an opportunity to write a book with several other authors, and I bought in because the manager of the project seemed credible. In the end, she stole all of our money, failing to provide any of the promised services. To this day, I still do not know what she did with it, but I know that my dignity was more important than the chance of getting it back, and that I could not allow her to continue taking advantage of me.

As a business owner, you will be offered many different opportunities. This is especially the case for marketing, where there are so many technologically-assisted methods available. Some of the opportunities you encounter will be in your field, and others will not; of this second group, some will be good for you solely because of the exposure benefits they provide.

As I scrolled through social media feeds one day, I saw an offer to write a book with several other authors. The topic of the book was the pitfalls and successes of entrepreneurship, specifically from the perspective of millennial entrepreneurs. I knew I was experienced enough to write on the topic, and that I could use the book to market my new personal brand. It was also an opportunity to learn process of self-publishing a book, something I had aspired to do but lacked the knowledge to pull off on my own. (Obviously, I learned a lot from that experience. Here we are!)

I decided to reach out to the group that was advertising the opportunity, relaying my interest. I was told how much money it would cost to be a part of the project, and was given several deadlines to help me to make my final decision. The first deadline would be when I had to turn in my portion of the book, the others were for editorial, formatting, and publishing services offered by the project manager, including deadlines for returning our edits and for the manuscript to be finalized. After corresponding with the project manager over email, I decided that this would be good for me and my brand.

Right away, I made several mistakes. My first mistake was paying the fee up front without ensuring I would receive something of value in return. At that time, the project included myself along with seven other authors. If I had known more about the self-publishing process back then, I would have been able to protect myself, but it was a new area for me and it was difficult to tell exactly what I was up against. In hindsight, it is clear that something was not right about the initial arrangement.

Within a week, one author dropped out of the project. My second mistake was not paying more attention at that time, and not asking questions about why they had done so. I chose to be generous instead, and to give the project the benefit of the doubt. I reasoned that life sometimes gets in the way, and that there could have been any number of reasons why this particular author decided against participating.

Fast forward a month and a half, and the first draft of my chapter was due. I was proud of my work, and was excited to click the "send" button on my email to the project manager. As a recovering perfectionist, I had changed the angle of my chapter many times, rewriting sections and changing details. I was ready to send it away, get it out of my hands and off my mind. I wanted it to be perfect, but I already knew that when writing non-fiction, there is never a "perfect" for me. I am a tough critic of my own work, and it is better for me to have a strong but imperfect product than to be paralyzed by self-criticism and end up not producing anything at all. I have dozens of projects sitting on my computer, or in my mind awaiting development, because I have not felt that they were at the level I wanted them to be. Writing has taught me that you just have to start, you just have to do it. You have to not judge yourself, and let the process be what it is. So, sitting in front of my computer, with a smile on my face, I clicked "send" with tremendous satisfaction.

Once I turned the chapter in, I got confirmation that the project manager had received my portion of the book. She told all the participating authors that the first round of edits would be given to us about a month and a half after later. The wait began. This was my third mistake: I did not follow up actively enough, did not monitor the project closely enough. Six weeks later, I had honestly forgotten about the book, when one of my co-authors brought to my attention that we were nearing the first deadline. We had not heard anything from the project manager since those first confirmation emails. We were surprised, as she had promised to walk us through the self-publishing process.

I posted a message of excitement to the private Facebook group she had created for the authors, saying how happy I was that we would be receiving the edits back the next day. I knew this would spark some conversation, and, indeed, as soon as I posted it the other authors jumped in to voice their excitement as well. The project manager came out of hiding and told us that our edits would be delayed, because her original editor had dropped the ball and she was working on another book project that took priority over ours. She told us that the edited drafts would not be returned to us for at least another month.

Of course, looking back, this was a major sign of trouble. When deadlines are not met by a project manager, it is always important to ask why. The deadline change also revealed the significance of my very first mistake; without a formal contract, we had no choice but to wait. None of us were pleased with the delay, because we paid our money in the understanding that project completion was tied to specific dates and that she would be teaching us the basics of self-publishing, only to receive NONE of the advertised services and miss the very first deadline.

In the period where out book was delayed, the project manager completed a different book with several other authors, advertised it, and held a book launch party for it. She regularly posted updated about activities done for her other businesses, including traveling out of the country to secure merchandise options for one of them. This was all very off-putting.

The next thing we knew, the second deadline came around, and still no edits had been returned to us. She claimed that they had, but we co-authors had kept in contact throughout the process, and none of us had received anything. This was the point where we all moved from frustration into suspecting that something was fishy about the whole arrangement. We had hoped to have our edits back already, and our books published and ready for sale during the November and December holiday season, but that was clearly not going to happen. She completed other projects, but seemed to be ignoring ours.

Moreover, she continued to be unresponsive. I decided to post my frustrations about the process in the private Facebook group. This was the right move, and something I should have done earlier: we had paid for education, editing, and publishing, and received none of it. This active follow-up was effective, and that same night, the project manager sent back my edited chapter. I did not look at it right away, because it was early in the morning when she sent it and I wanted to give the edits my full attention. When I finished with my obligations that day, I sat down to read the revised text. Now, a central part of the project plan was that a professional editor would be hired to edit our drafts. So I was shocked to find, upon reviewing the document, that the project manager had edited my chapter herself. The editor that she allegedly submitted our money to had not even touched my chapter.

I persisted in my active approach, confronting the project manager about this. She became defensive and would not explain what had happened. I could not understand why someone with such a good reputation, and so much influence, would take advantage of people.

Be willing to walk away if something is not serving you

I made some of my co-authors aware of what was happening, and everyone was understandably upset. The majority of them had still not received the edits for their portions of the book, and were forced to question the credibility of our project manager. All but two of us decided to walk away from the project.

Of course, the project manager blamed me for this. She took no ownership of how she had damaged the project and failed to deliver services that had been promised and paid for. I wrote to her asking for a refund, and she refused. She replied that we had all been well-aware that there would be no refunds should we decide not to go through with the project. Her statement was not true. I provided every document she ever gave us, including the document she used to advertise the opportunity. Nowhere did it say, "no refunds." She then claimed that because the editor had already been paid, and because she made no money from the project, that there was nothing left to refund to us. I did not believe that either, as there was no evidence of an outside editor having been involved at any stage.

However, I knew that when I walked away there was a chance I would be unable to recover the money I had already spent. It was worth it to me to leave rather than continue to be lied to. It was more worthwhile to walk away than to continue putting my faith in a person who could not or would not deliver on her promises.

This bring me to my next point, which is the importance of protecting yourself with reputable, reliable systems. Had I used a system like the one I chose for this book, I would have been in a very different

situation, with the guarantee of getting what I expected from the project.

Protect yourself with reputable systems

As an attorney, I should have known better than to do business with

someone without signing a hard contract with them in advance. I was

misled by the fact that the project manager happened to be an attorney as

well, so I felt I could trust her because she and I were both held to the

same ethical standards in other areas of our work. What the experience

taught me is that you cannot offer that level of trust to anyone when you

are doing business. Contract, contract, contract!

Even more generally, when I started the journey of the collaborative

book project, I did not go through a reputable system in order to protect

myself. Having learned from that experience, I found my editor for this

book project through a reputable company online. The company had

systems in place that ensured that both myself and the editor were

protected during our business relationship. For instance, the money I

agreed to pay was placed in escrow rather than delivered immediately.

(What this means is that the money was set aside into an account controlled by a third party, and released only when both of us agreed that the work was completed.)

This arrangement protected both myself and the editor in case our business relationship did not work out. As certain milestones of the process were completed, the editor was able to be paid from escrow, subject to my approval of the work. I had the right to review the work before paying him, and he had the protection of an appeals and review process.

Similar protections will always be available to you, whether you go through a reputable third party or use well-written contracts and trust in small claims courts, the Better Business Bureau, and other methods of consumer protection to ensure the contract's effectiveness. The lesson here is: use the systems available to you.

Have a clear vision

I had a clear vision of what I wanted to use the book for. It would be a marketing opportunity for me that would help to solidify my reputation as a knowledgeable and trustworthy consultant. Books are investments of your time, money, and effort, so you want to have a plan to capitalize off of all your hard work.

I had intended to have a book launch once the book was finished, as part of building the book into my business. I had already contacted several people about being part of the event. I had been worried that the project manager might not produce the final produce in time for my launch, and my worries were realized. I made the decision to walk away prior to losing any additional money on booking a venue and other incidental costs associated with event planning. By leaving when I did, I also avoided the cost of ordering books in print. The financial consequences from the failed book project could easily have spiraled out of control, but I was honest with myself and was able to cut my losses.

My other, underlying goal for that project had been to understand the process of self-publishing a book. I did not learn this in the way I had imagined. However, I followed up on that plan, and the failed project did set me on a path to learning what I needed to know. This book is self-published. I walked away from that deal because it was the best thing to do, both morally and to protect my pocketbook.

How to recover from mistakes

It is not always easy to recover from mistakes. So, how would one know when to walk away from a deal? Here are some tips to help you recognize these situations for yourself. First, know your deal breakers. Set boundaries through a contract. Know exactly what lines you will not cross and will not tolerate being crossed. Second, go with your gut, and be proactive. If you feel that something is off, it probably is. There is never anything wrong with doing some research and asking questions. That will let you find out whether what you are feeling is just your fears trying to talk you out of something amazing, or a real red flag. Once you have gathered enough information to know that you are feeling something more than just fear, you will know whether your spirit is telling you that there is something you should be paying attention to or looking out for. Do not ignore that warning. Finally, decide whether the return on investment is worth it to you, whether what you are putting in to the project is worth what you expect to get out of it. Write out a list of pros and cons; confer with trusted sources; ask lots of questions. Ultimately, you are responsible for protecting your business, and if you do not, no one else will.

Reflect and Write

What are your deal breakers when it comes to doing business with people?

Have you ever entered into a deal that you regretted?

Did you walk away from it? If not, what would it have taken for you to walk away?

Do you make sure all of your business dealings are governed by legally binding contracts?

What can you do to protect yourself in future business dealings?

Chapter 8: Pursue Your Passions

One of the fastest ways to change your life is to
pursue your passions.

Your chances of mastering entrepreneurship greatly improve when your

business is based on something you are passionate about. Because

entrepreneurship is such a rollercoaster journey, doing something you are

passionate about can sometimes be the key to being able to stick with it

rather than having to give up. Sometimes, your driving passion is the

only thing you have left to rely on when things are not going the way you

envisioned. You want your business to be something that makes you

excited to get out of bed in the morning.

Some people do not know what they are passionate about, while

others have multiple passions and have to choose which they want to

pursue. No matter which end of the spectrum you fall on, it will be

important to understand which passions are for you alone, and which passions you can use in the service of others. Passions you can rely on in the service of others will serve you best in entrepreneurship, while the others could quickly lead you into poverty.

I heard a sermon by Pastor Keith Battle years ago, in which he said that one way to find your passion is to consider what frustrates you. I have found that statement to be true, for both personal passions and service-related passions. Personal passions are the ones you use just for yourself, or your hobbies, relationships, and dreams. Service-related passions are ones you can use in the service of others, and are the ones you should seek in your entrepreneurial journeys.

Many things frustrate each of us about this world and how it operates. Sometimes, under the surface of that frustration is a fire of wanting to do something about it, along with the inherent capability to do so.

No passion = the beginning of the end

When I opened my law practice in 2012, it was more out of necessity than it was out of passion. As a result, I found myself on the verge of burnout more times than I can count. I was not getting proper rest, and

I did not find the legal areas I was practicing interesting. My motivation for starting the firm was to simply to make ends meet, in the hope that my business would grow to a point where I would not have to think about how my bills would be paid every month. That arrangement was unsustainable.

But it was not all without passion. I did take an interest in some areas of practice. In particularly, I found business law and estate planning interesting. Now, ever since I can remember, I have always been full of brilliant ideas. I may be biased when I say that, but I often have business concepts and ideas; they come to me easily, almost in an instant. Dreaming or awake, I have business ideas. So, when I noticed that I had a passion for business and business law, and found myself always giving people advice about business and how it worked, I realized that I had the ingredients of a passion-driven business. I was giving free advice to people when I could have been charging; it was time to change.

What you do for free may be your passion

Pastor Battle gave us one way to find your passion, which is to find what frustrates you. Another is to figure out what you would be willing to do for free. Everyone should explore both of these ways of finding their passion, both personal and service-related. Helping people brainstorm about their businesses, refine ideas, plan, and get the appropriate groundwork laid is something I both enjoy and look forward to. I enjoyed the early process of building my business so much, that back in 2012 I applied and was chosen for a position as an adjunct professor at a local community college, where I taught business law to paralegals.

Estate planning is a different story. Estate planning is the work you do to prepare for death or incapacitation. This includes wills, trusts, advanced health directives for end-of-life care and care when incapacitated, powers of attorney, and guardianship for minor children or children with special needs. I have not always been drawn to this subject matter, because, frankly, it can be desperately sad to think about death and incapacitation. Additionally, the droves of paperwork that often need to completed, and with perfect precision, can be daunting. Misplacing just one word could mean the difference between someone receiving a gift that a friend or relative willed to them, or not. Talk about pressure! I found my passion for estate planning only through trying to assist members of my generation with planning for their own families' legacies.

This was my experience. I felt frustrated after seeing many people suffering through hardship and adversity after the deaths of loves ones. It was difficult seeing people unable to inherit anything, or pass anything down to their families so that future generations could benefit. I wanted so badly to tell people that planning could be the cure to many of these problems, even if they did not have many assets. Having a simple plan is always better than having no plan at all! My mother used to tell me, "If you do not have a plan, you plan to fail"; planning for death is no different.

This time around, I have been able to succeed in business because I discovered my service-related passion. I noticed that I really enjoy educating people and helping them to build the lives that they dream of by pursuing entrepreneurial careers. Learning to break down the legal information involved in a relatable way has been challenging, but rewarding.

However, I have found that despite my hard work, there are certain things that people prioritize over planning for death. People will happily plan for babies, marriages, and buying homes, but often will not take the extra step of planning for the care of their children, partners, and assets in the event that something should happen to them. This is dispiriting. Sometimes I have wanted to give up, and change my service offerings, targeting a demographic that is already in the market. Yet, I hesitate, wondering whether I could be happy abandoning the group I am most passionate about reaching. As of now, I still work to make that aspect of my business relatable to Generation X and Millennials, but have adjusted my expectations as to the feedback I will receive in that quest, and have become more open to providing services that are in higher demand.

Fresh ideas as a fruit of passion

When you pursue your passion, it is much easier to come up with fresh ideas to make your business better. It is also much easier to re-invent yourself if need be. I have changed the lines in my Instagram profile more often than I can remember, but not because anything is wrong. On that contrary! It is because, as my business grows, I am refining what I do and how I market my brand. I am going back to the drawing board whenever I need to. I am taking inventory of what I am selling and what I want people to know me for. Thanks to my passion for my work, I actually enjoy taking the time to brainstorm ideas about my business, and plan out how to make those ideas come to fruition.

Greater work ethic and sacrifice as a fruit of passion

When you pursue passion, you are also likely to work harder and longer when you need to. Ever worked at a job you hated? It can be incredibly difficult to put the effort into something that you do not enjoy. It is much easier to sacrifice your time or energy for something you are passionate about. There have been moments where I have had to wake up early or stay up late to get things done. I have had to spend lots of money to buy office supplies, to pay for marketing, and to purchase web domains and website development. In entrepreneurship, there will always be a level of sacrifice required, so make sure that whatever your business is, you are passionate about it.

At this point in my career, I am still employed full-time by a larger law company. However, the money I make from that work helps to fund my business. I will continue doing this until my business grows enough to support me working for myself full-time.

I have noticed a dramatic change in my life since I took a leap of faith and tried entrepreneurship a second time. My confidence has grown because I enjoy what I am doing, and because I am good at it. My life feels more fulfilled because I am working in the service of others, helping them realize their dreams and plan for something as important as death. I have noticed that I do not tire of what I am doing as quickly as I did when I was a solo practitioner the first time around, because, for the most part, I enjoy the day-to-day activities of my business. Sometimes, I sit and work on my business for several hours without noticing how late it is.

More motivation to overcome obstacles

When you pursue your passion, nothing will stop you. The cycle of obstacles that you have to overcome in entrepreneurship is much easier to persevere through when you are passionate about what you are doing. When I had my first law practice in 2012, I was passionate about paying my bills, not practicing. And, of course, there are many ways to pay your bills. So it is easy to understand why, after a year had gone by and with so many obstacles between me and entrepreneurial success, I scaled back and found another source of income.

Currently, I am using my full-time job to fund my business until I have enough sources of income to work for myself on a full-time basis. I work almost ten-hour days at that job, and have another two hours of commuting time every day. That means twelve hours out of each day are devoted to my full-time position. Only after I get off work am I able to spend my extra time growing my business, doing things like writing this book, thinking things through, and making my business what I truly want it to be. I would not be able to do that, or work this hard, if I was not passionate about what I am building.

As you can see, half of each weekday is devoted to working for someone else. You probably endure a similar situation. Since most of our lives will be spent working, why not work for ourselves doing something we enjoy? Some people are beginning to define this kind of happiness as "the new wealth." As my business grows and I experience what life is like working for myself, I see the truth of that statement. I find that I am at my best when I am doing things I am passionate about.

(This paragraph is a brief detour from the main themes of this chapter. I want you to truly understand that in business, and in pursuing your passions, you need to enter into it with your eyes open. Before you take the leap of pursuing your passion, understand that just because it is something you care about deeply does not mean it is something that will make you lots of money. For all the reasons just reviewed, it is likely to do so, but there are no guarantees. I have seen some very interesting business concepts meet with unlikely success, so I will not try make a list of things that are unlikely to be profitable or sustainable. However, I will tell you to do your research. In particular, market studies are one of the best ways to figure out whether there is demand for the product or service that you want to sell.)

You add more value to yourself and the world when you pursue your passion. You will naturally think harder, work longer, and put your all into it. As a result of that, you will deliver a service or product that is much more valuable than if it were something you were doing just to make a living, or because you were obligated to.

You can pursue passions you are not skilled at

Weigh out the pros and cons of pursuing your passion. Are you particularly skilled at the thing you are passionate about? If not, you still have two options that will let you to pursue your passion, as long as you have the patience for them and plan ahead. First, you can build your skills. That might mean practicing on the side, taking night classes, working with a mentor who will ensure that you know the proper way to do things, or maybe even going back to school full-time, if you can afford to. Take the time you need to hone your craft, and slowly work your way up to starting a business with it.

The second way you can pursue passions you are not particularly skilled at is to hire other people that are skilled in what you want to do. You could manage the company and oversee the work, so long as you do not mind having a less involved, hands-on approach to your company. Keep in mind, though, that managing also requires skill. If you are not a skilled manager, you can also hire a project manager who specializes in the area you want to build your business in, and take the opportunity to learn from them over time. Either way, make sure you plan out your chosen course of action well in advance!

Reflect and Write

What are you passionate about?

If you're unsure of what you are passionate about, what issue or problem frustrates you?

Is your passion something that will assist with the service of others?

If not, how can you tailor your passion to fulfill a need?

What is the purpose behind starting your business?

Chapter 9. The Importance of Your Circle and Network

"Your network is your net worth." Unknown

The power of positive networks

Moguls have gotten this down to a science. If you look at the people they spend time around and do business with, they mostly have the same goals and upward trajectory. If your network is not doing anything or going anywhere, then chances are you are not either. I worked for years trying to figure out what I needed to do to get to the next level in my life and in my businesses. It turns out the old adage, "it's not what you know, but who you know" is true!

I have some of the most wonderful and supportive friends and family in the world, but no one in my immediate circle was an entrepreneur, nor were any of them in my profession. In fact, none of them had the time to chase their dreams the way I was chasing mine. I found myself at a standstill, unsure of how to progress. I thought that if I could just work hard enough, somehow what I wanted would eventually materialize.

That was partially true, but I came to realize that you have to surround yourself with a specific group of people if you really want to take your business to another level. You need a team of people who can help you, who have done before what you are doing now, or who, at the very least, have been entrepreneurs for a while and can give you advice about being in business.

In 2017, I decided that I would launch a new business. A personal brand. Part of what I wanted to do was market myself in such a way that I could create passive streams of income. One way to do that is by writing books. Once the books are published and available for purchase, they can sell themselves while you sleep if you market them properly. In Chapter 7, I shared with you the story of the first failed book project I was a part of, but I did not tell you what it led me to, or how it got me there.

At the end of 2017, I was searching for a photographer to take photos of me for the book cover. I recalled a former classmate and friend of mine whose mother was an amazing photographer. I reached out to this friend and asked whether her mother still shot photos for people. I was told that, yes, she did, and was given the information to get in touch. When I made contact with the photographer, I was greeted warmly and asked what I needed. I relayed my goals and hopes for the project, and we set a date to have the photoshoot. The day itself turned out to be unseasonably warm for December, as I set out to take headshots and some other photos for the book. As I drove up to the photography studio, I found myself immediately in awe of what I saw. Unbeknownst to me, I was approaching the studio and home of a nationally known photographer, who just so happened to be the mother of someone I went to high school with, and who lived only twenty minutes away from me!

When I arrived, she escorted me into her studio to get my makeup done. There, I was greeted by an amazing makeup artist. I was grateful—you would have had to be amazing to cover up the huge pimple that had formed on my forehead just that morning. She took her time working on my face, and we chatted as she did. She asked me what I was taking the pictures for, and I discovered that she was looking to start her own business. We exchanged information; as a lawyer who practices business law, I was more than happy to help if she needed me.

Once my makeup was finished, I was led into a room to get ready for the first outfit change (I had three planned). The house was, architecturally, a circle. From the end of one room, you could not see into the next. I had never seen anything quite like it, yet I was drawn to its clean, white spaciousness.

I was then led into another room to take the first round of photos. The photographer asked me, as she worked, what I hoped to do in my future and whether I had any mentors. She ran through a long list of names she could connect me with, and, sure enough, while we were looking through some of the finished pictures, she called one of them. A day later, I was in contact with a trailblazing woman who would become my new mentor.

Little did I know then that the day after the shoot, the same day I would connect with my new mentor, would be the same day the book project came crashing to a halt. The only reason I had gone to take the photos in the first place would no longer exist. It was not a waste of time, though; on the contrary, although that first book never came out, I was able to start relationships with several women who would help me carry the project forward. We decided to stay connected and to carry on what we had begun. One of the women was able to recruit several other women knowledgeable about printing and publishing, and together we were able to publish this book just over a year after the first project started.

The mentor I mentioned above is not a lawyer, but she has certainly been in business much longer than I have. Not only has she been an entrepreneur for almost two decades, she is an accomplished author and publisher, and was able to shepherd me through the process of self-publishing this book, from start to finish. She taught me the ins and outs of the self-publishing process, as well as the importance of marketing myself and the book so that it could be successful. Books do not become best sellers by chance; they become best sellers thanks to the work you put in and the way you intentionally position yourself in the market. And the chances are that unless you are a famous celebrity who has gone through a traditional publisher, you will not have the exposure needed to automatically make you a best-selling author. This means you have to put the work in, set clear goals, and position yourself to get the exposure you need. In other words, my mentor gave me the information I needed to avoid future mistakes in the publishing game. Information that would have been oh-so-helpful to me just a few months earlier.

With all the information my mentor gave me, I was made aware that I would need to put together a public relations campaign if I wanted to ensure the success of my solo book project. I was able to make contact with someone I have admired since I was a child, who also happens to run her own public relations firm. We ran into one another at a funeral, and I was able to discuss with her what I was trying to do.

(Never forget that a chance encounter, even at a funeral, is much easier to have than a carefully-solicited informational interview.)

She gladly agreed to meet with me on a professional basis. During our first few meetings, I noticed that a lot of the information given to me by my mentor was being repeated by this public relations guru. This was very encouraging—whenever you are taking advice from people, make sure you check your sources. My sources knew what they were talking about, having had so many years in their respective businesses, so I was definitely going to take their advice; the fact that they agreed just demonstrated that I was lucky to have such valuable support.

One of the things I noticed very quickly was that I was connected to more people than I realized. I was not effectively utilizing my network. Makeup artists and photographers, by the very nature of what they do, have more connections than almost anyone else. There is a high chance that some of those people have achieved exactly what you want to achieve, or have been exactly where you want to go. Once I realized that

I was connected to so many people, I brainstormed ways that those connections could be used as resources to help me on my journey. I was able to utilize many of them, and, in some cases, I had already been doing so without recognizing it.

For instance, I decided to host a "Women in Business" panel a month into my first book project. I know several women with their own businesses from different walks of life, and I was able to host the panel at a local library. One panelist was a social media influencer, another an attorney with her own law practice, and a third owned of her own technology company. All were women I had known and been connected to for years.

I have also been working to expand my network, and it has paid off tremendously. Almost every time you meet a new person is a networking opportunity. Always keep your business cards on you and be ready to offer them; you never know when you might meet a person who could be key to bringing your business to the next level. Meeting my mentor and re-connecting with the public relations manager both happened by chance, not thanks to head-hunting. In other words, having an upwardly mobile network is much more helpful than having to go out and create connections deliberately, in a targeted manner. You find people easily, quickly, and without investing work when you can rely on organic business relationships that you already have.

Negative networks: Avoiding toxic relationships

> If you've seen a mogul with toxic relationships, you've seen a mogul who is living below their potential.

Every time in my life when I have been living below my potential, I have also been in negative relationships that were draining the life out of me. Every type of relationship you have will involve experiences of adversity in some shape or form. What makes all the differences is how you handle them as they come along.

The first and only time I nearly failed a course in college was because of a relationship that was negatively affecting my energy. Over just a few months I lost thirty pounds, and I had a hard time putting the weight back on, due to the toxicity in my circle of friends and acquaintances. It took me years to remove that toxicity from my life. There were times during that period when I did not want to leave the bed, times I could not be bothered with people, and times I forced myself to sleep instead of tending to my obligations. All of those feelings can be traced back the toxicity in my relationships that was draining my energy. I was still able to function, but only just barely. It is impossible to perform your best when you are feeling your worst.

Moguls are often surrounded by people who admire them, who are inspired by them, or who are just plain old leeches and opportunists. A lot of them are there because people want what moguls have, or are hoping to emulate them or replicate their success. Then there are those who are just lazy, and want to take advantage of anything they can get from the *mogul* without putting in any actual work to improve their own lives. Relationships with other people can be complicated, but when you are trying to get to the next level in your life, or business, you have to simplify and try to make things as straightforward and uplifting as possible. The more energy you spend on things that are draining you, the less you will have to offer to your business, or to positive connections in your life. Now, crucially, in no way do I suggest neglecting your relationships. What I do suggest is evaluating the relationships you have. Make sure you understand how they are affecting you. Some relationships are totally worth fighting for and worth the extra energy; however, there are some relationships that just suck the life right out of you.

An example of a relationship that is likely not worth hanging onto is one that takes more from you than they give back. You know, the ones where someone only calls you when they need something. Or the relationships where someone calls you with their problems over and over, refusing to take the solutions you have offered more than once. You may want to re-evaluate those relationships. In general, if a relationship takes energy from you without offering anything back—if it is completely one-sided—you should steer clear of it or remove yourself from it entirely. You need to cut those relationships out of your life if you are serious about reaching the next level in your entrepreneurship journey. You cannot run a marathon carrying weight on your back, the you cannot start a company carrying toxic connections. Eventually the weight will become too heavy, and you will have to either let it go or let it cause you to fail and not finish your "race."

What about the relationships where you are unsure, where they just do not feel quite right? Discernment and intuitions about relationships matter. Trust yourself. Sometimes you just know you deserve better than the treatment you are getting, and in those instances, it is always a good idea to remove those relationships from your life, or reduce their influence. The more you let yourself settle for harmful relationships, the more of your confidence you will sacrifice. Of course, feelings can lead you astray sometimes, and it is okay to seek out the root of why you feel what you feel, but remember to be true to yourself. If any relationship causes you to second-guess your value, it is time to let it go.

Sometimes, making these choices is unbelievably hard. Sometimes the very people we want to bring with us on our journeys are the ones holding us back. It can be one of the most difficult things to accept and digest as an entrepreneur, but it is part of the process of becoming the successful *mogul* you want so much to be.

Through the process of becoming an entrepreneur and seeking continual growth for your business, you will learn who your true friends are, who really has your back, who you can trust, and, hopefully, you will learn the importance of detachment. We often become so attached to the people in our lives that we have a hard time letting go, even when the relationships have run their course.

Your ability to let go of toxic relationships will ultimately determine how far you can run. Your ability to choose your circle wisely will ensure you go farther than you ever dreamed you could.

Reflect and Write

Does your circle have the same mindset as you? (If not, you may want to start to expand.)

Do you have people in your circle who are further along in their business journey than you are? Who are they?

Do you have a mentor in your field? If not, begin to look for someone who might be able to connect with a possible mentor.

Do you effectively utilize your network? If not, identify some people you know or have met that you can use as a resource as you build your business.

How do your closest relationships make you feel?

Do your relationships give back to you, in energy, affirmation, or support?

Do any of your relationships raise red flags for you? If so, why do you think that might be?

Name two people you would like to connect to within the next month, and set up appointments to meet with them.

Chapter 10. Take Care of Yourself

If you are already a person who has a difficult time finding balance and prioritizing, becoming a business owner will just add to this challenge.

Self-care tips for entrepreneurs

Moguls take care of themselves. I lost 30 pounds in three months without dieting or exercising. I am not looking for recognition for this. It was a horrible situation I found myself in. I was not trying to lose weight, and it only happened because of high stress levels and a lack of self-care.

Here are tips for self-care to help you to succeed in entrepreneurship. Of course, they're important outside of starting a business as well, and we can all use them right now, but in this context, they are important advice for growing entrepreneurs.

Be good to your best friend, you

After some difficult life situations, a good girlfriend of mine shared some advice with me. She had been told by her counselor to treat herself the way she would treat her best friend. That sentiment stuck with me. We often treat ourselves so harshly, and neglect ourselves so much, that we cannot even claim to love ourselves. How do we end up treating our friends so much better than ourselves? This revelation came to me years after I needed it most, in law school, but it was a timely lesson nonetheless.

Through my years in college and law school, and the years since, I have learned several ways to practice self-care. There is no way you can successfully run a business or become the *mogul* you wish to be without taking care of yourself.

When I think of business ownership, one of the first things I think about is how much work it can be. When do business owners have time to take care of themselves? And, if they work a traditional nine to five position and spend time with their business only afterwards, it gets even more difficult to find time for self-care. It is a challenge that each business owner ends up facing at one point or another. If you are already someone who has a difficult time finding balance and prioritizing, becoming a business owner will just add to your struggle.

Due to the social climate we all live in, and the importance of mental health, I am going to spend some extra love and care on this chapter in the hope that you will be able to use some of these tips as you experience the journey of entrepreneurship. Entrepreneurs work so hard, and this is a very important aspect of succeeding in business. In fact, it is arguably the most important one of all, because your business cannot succeed without you operating at your best, and that requires taking care of your health and well-being.

Always be intentional about self-care

I remember the first time I was faced with the challenge of balancing life and self-care, during my first year in law school. By now you know a lot of my story from back then. I was so stressed-out, and feared failing so much, that I studied all the time and hardly did anything else. I would go to campus early for my classes, and stay at school so long that I would end up watching the sunset from the warm attic in the library, just below the condemned spaces where bats lived. Pitiful, right? Most nights, I left campus after dark, only to go home and study some more.

Very rarely did I take the time to eat a decent meal. When I ate lunch, I usually opted for something light, like soup and a salad, so as to not make myself tired during the day. I would often have broccoli and cheese soup and a salad. That was my go-to. My roommate would see me during the day and ask if I was losing weight. It got back enough that she once asked whether I was throwing up my food, and I could only assure that her I was not. I was totally oblivious to the weight loss and did not notice that my clothes were getting too big for my body. My mind was focused solely on remaining in school and getting my grades up.

When I came home for Thanksgiving break, my parents barely recognized me. I went to school at 132 pounds just three months prior, and came home for the holiday break weighing 102. My parents, sisters, and friends were worried about me, and did what they could. I remember everyone watching me as I ate my Thanksgiving dinner, wanting to be sure I was eating. As my fork went to the plate to bring food back up toward my mouth, their eyes followed my every movement.

I found out later that they thought I had gone away to school and developed an eating disorder, just as my roommate had alluded. That was not the case. My survival instincts kicked in, the "fight or flight" reflex as it is sometimes called, and I was in pure "fight" mode. I was so hyper-focused on the tasks at hand—studying, bringing my grades up—that nothing else mattered, not even meals. That may sound extreme, but it was my story.

I was driven by a keen, cutting awareness of the danger I was in, and the constant risk that I would be kicked out of school. I ended up being kicked out of school anyway, and pushed myself to persevere through that, too.

In hindsight, I should have taken much better care of myself. I did very well in school that next semester, but there is a strong chance that I could have done far better if I was healthier in mind and body. I would have had more energy, an easier time focusing, and better sleep. I still struggle with this very thing when I get stressed, but these days I do a better job recognizing what is happening and make sure to eat consistent meals, so that the stress on my body and mind is not so extreme.

Faith as self-care

My faith was, and is, of utmost importance to me. So much so that I started a Bible study in law school, and held it out of my home. I did not know anyone, but I was determined to stay committed to the active practice of my faith, even hundreds of miles away from home. My faith was the only thing that kept me going, when everything else seemed to be falling apart. Many people rely on their faith or religion to get them through hard times. For me, holding onto faith let me hold on to hope, and that kept me going when I wanted to give up. I cried myself to sleep so many times. I prayed while I worked out on the elliptical. My roommate and I prayed together sometimes too. Eventually, some other classmates started coming to the Bible study I held, and we would pray for one another and connect through our shared experience of faith. Due to my demanding class and study schedule, I eventually set aside my own Bible study, and instead attended one held by the school. They would serve food, and it meant that I did not have to prepare the messages—I could simply arrive ready to participate. I no longer had the time nor energy to devote to preparation, so it was a good fit. Oh, and did I mention that the food was home cooked by our professors and their wives? How could I pass that up?

Get physical

Exercising is another great way to practice self-care. I discovered a mild love for exercise during school. It was not as helpful as it could have been, given that I was not eating properly, but it was still therapeutic. I had been a dancer for most of my childhood and was very athletic, so being away at school without my normal physical activities was a huge adjustment, and one that took a toll on my body and my energy. I discovered distance running, something I had never imagined being able to do. I was always a short distance runner, a sprinter, so distance was a challenge at first. I got into it because being able to listen to my music on longer runs and just think about nothing but that current moment helped to clear my mind. I even ran a couple of 5ks, which was a huge accomplishment for me. I also noticed that getting my medals at the end of races was just a bit addictive—but that's another story for another day.

Eat, and eat right

Eating properly as part of self-care might seem like a no-brainer, but it is something that most of us do not have a good grasp of. On my busy days, I still reach for whatever food is quick and easy, even if it is not the healthiest. On your busiest days is exactly when your body needs balanced nutrition most. Your brain literally needs these nutrients to fuel it. Without them, you cannot think clearly, cannot coordinate your movements, cannot even focus your attention.

I was told that the brain only has a certain amount of energy that it consumes each day, and once it reaches that level, it will not exert any more effort. Your brain looks for ways to preserve your energy, not deplete it. Your body will begin to compensate for the lack of energy available to it in other ways, starting to shut down non-vital processes. You will stay on your feet, but you will not be operating at your full potential. So: keep a healthy snack at hand, and prepare your meals in advance. If you do not have to time to do that, try to make the time. It will save you money and calories, and keep you functioning well.

Quiet time and meditation

Quiet time and meditation as a form of self-care has become something I value more and more. Some people equate meditation with prayer, and that can be right. But sometimes, just being quiet and taking a moment to breathe can be therapeutic all on its own. I remember that when I took the bar exam, all twelve hours of it, one of the ways I was able to reset my mind—other than going to the restroom and doing jumping jacks—was to close my eyes and breathe in deeply for five seconds. I would repeat that exercise over and over for a full minute, and would then continue with the test.

Meditation often involves deep breathing, but it does not have to. Sometimes it is just taking the time to think about the things you are grateful for. Sometimes it is repeating affirmations to yourself. Sometimes it can be reciting scripture or thinking about something positive—an image, phrase, or memory. Meditation can be many things. Personally, I like to either turn on music and let myself sit quietly, or go out into nature. I love being by the water or in the mountains. There is something impossibly peaceful about hearing the waves crash against the shore, or the river trickling between the rocks under its surface. It is so calming to hear birds chirp, and wind blow through the leaves, all without worrying about answering an email or phone call.

Some people use guided meditations. You can find these in yoga classes or through digital media platforms like YouTube. A simple search for "guided meditation" will lead you to almost any type of meditation you might like, whether you like visualization, rhythmic breathing, paying attention to your body and environment, or something else entirely.

Built-in celebration

A lot of entrepreneurs, like myself, are accomplishment-driven. We work so hard and run so fast trying to accomplish our goals that we often fail to take the time to acknowledge what we achieve. We pass each success by in our rush to reach the next. I graduated law school eight years ago, and still have not taken the time to properly celebrate that achievement. I graduated, went home, and immediately started to study for the bar exam. When I passed the bar, I did not have a proper celebration for that, either. Maybe one day I will celebrate all my accomplishments at the same time, in one massive party.

Sleep

Rest is important. It is difficult to do much of anything without proper rest. Lack of sleep makes it difficult to concentrate, and it is almost impossible to be productive if you cannot focus. I do not miss pulling all-nighters in school, going without sleep for a full twenty-four hours. Running a business is hard work, and sometimes it requires making it through the day with little sleep, but I have yet to experience a night where I got none at all.

But let me be real here. If you work a full-time job, and run a business after work, it is going to be almost impossible to get the prescribed amount of sleep. I lost the ability to sleep for eight hours straight long ago, but I still know when to slow down, or call it quits, because I really need to rest. For instance, if I notice that I have just read the same sentence three or four times, and its meaning is just not registering, then I know that I either need to rest, or take a deep breath to reset. Usually, I just need to rest for a while.

So, how do we get around sleep deprivation? Create a schedule where you build in your rest, one that you can live with. Remember that rest looks different for each person. There is nothing wrong with committing to a bed time, or at least to a time where you unplug from your electronic devices.

What about your friends?

Human interaction is so important. Spending time with friends and loved ones is a crucial way to take care of yourself. Laughter is a wonderful way to wind down and relieve stress. I used to surf the internet regularly to find funny skits or videos and share them with my loved ones, helping all of us laugh. It really helps! Going to your favorite restaurant, dancing (also great physical activity!), and just being around others who genuinely enjoy your company, all can recharge and relax you.

It can be easy to become lonely when you are pushing hard to build and run your business. Businesses take up large amounts of time, if you are not careful, they can take it all. It is easy for your friendships and relationships to suffer, if you are not intentional about maintaining them. The stress on relationships caused by entrepreneurship is a very real thing, and when your relationships are stressed and tense, you as an individual will carry that stress around with you. You will need to help your loved ones understand what you are doing, and why, and how it affects your time, in order for your relationships with them to remain healthy.

What do you love?

Ultimately, try to incorporate things you love into your daily routine. This is one of the best ways to ensure you are taking care of yourself, and to build self-care into your other tasks and responsibilities. For myself, I love music. I make it a point to listen to the music that I love, every day. I love my family, so I make it a point to speak with at least one of them, every day. I love good food, and while I should probably cut back on the amount of good food I eat, I have at least been eating well while I have been writing this book. I love feeling good about myself. What are some things that make me feel good about myself? Getting my hair done, getting my nails done, helping other people, accomplishing small day-to-day tasks. Of course, I those are not daily activities, but there are certainly other things I can do—positive affirmation, meditation—to feel good about myself every day.

Hobbies are an important example of what I am talking about here: things you enjoy doing, that both relax you and give you a sense of achievement. I find that reading or learning something new can be therapeutic. I like taking the time to learn a new song on my keyboard, for instance. The process of learning the music, and repeating it over and over until I progress, feels rewarding and gives me a space to be me, free from judgment. What does that for you?

You cannot function at your best if you are not taking care of yourself, and you cannot give anything to others if you have nothing left to give. Entrepreneurs are at much greater risk of burnout than other people are, because we often feel the responsibility to get everything done ourselves, right away, and as well as possible. We are not the best at taking care of ourselves, and often find it difficult to stay motivated to give ourselves care, with so many things to do and with so many responsibilities to manage. Finding the time is worth it, though: if we do not take care of ourselves, we just perpetuate a cycle that is unhealthy for us, which in turn will be unhealthy for our businesses and our relationships with the people around us.

Reflect and Write

What are some things you can do to prioritize exercise or build it into your routine?

What are some things you enjoy doing?

What are some things that make you feel good about yourself, which you can incorporate into your daily life?

What are some ways you can improve your eating habits?

How can you be a better communicator with your loved ones, especially about the demands of your business and your relationships with them?

What are some ways you can build rest into your routine or schedule?

Take-Home Lessons

Becoming a *mogul* does not require following a special formula. It does not require having every physical resource that you need to "make it" already available to you at the beginning. What it does require is a vision, a plan of action, lots of hard work, consistency in working on your business, discipline to maintain that consistency, attentiveness to nurture growth, and for you to take care of yourself along the way. I am well on my way to becoming a mogul, just as you will be if you apply the knowledge you have learned as you read this book, reflect on the prompts, and think about how my story relates to your own.

Knowing who you are

We have learned how important it is to know who you are, and how that shapes and frames your business identity. We have learned that when you know who you are, it is harder for outside influences to pressure you and control you. The same is true for your brand and business. We have learned that your business identity will determine how effectively you can stand out and set yourself apart from your competition. Everything you do with your business should ultimately tie directly in to your business identity as you have defined it. We learned that defining your business clearly helps you identify your target audience, which is one of the most important ingredients to starting a successful business. Never be afraid to stand out by being different!

Believe in yourself

Self- doubt and the trap of comparison can negatively affect both you and your business. We learned that people are buying based on their perceptions of us, not just our products. We learned that charging people less for services and products than you know they are worth, or failing to protect your business, reveal low self-esteem and a low opinion of your own work. We learned that one way we can boost our confidence is by facing our fears, and that the more risks we take, the higher our confidence will become. We learned that highlighting the skills, education, credentials, and uniqueness or creativity that make our businesses stand out can give us the edge we need to succeed.

Inner work

This is the part of business, and of life, that no one likes to talk about. But, we did it! We learned that entrepreneurship is full of obstacles, so much so that the journey of entrepreneurship will very often feel like a cycle of obstacles that must be overcome. We learned that one of the elements required to consistently move forward and upward is our focus. We learned that we must protect our energy. We learned that the narratives we accept about ourselves are the ones that matter most, and that affect us most deeply. We learned that we can use our failures to motivate us, to push us forward and focus our efforts. We learned that when our options are narrowed by adversity, it is also an opportunity to become creative, and to find new paths forward. Sometimes it takes time to overcome the negative things we have come to believe about ourselves. Sometimes it can feel like the situations we find ourselves in will never change, could never change, but they do change when we meet them with the right attitude and focus.

Persist and persevere

Because entrepreneurship can be a cycle of obstacles, success depends on your ability to persist and persevere. We learned that it is almost inevitable that you will be told "no," and that when you are, it is crucial not to internalize that rejection but to keep trying. Sometimes, in order to keep trying, you have to re-invent yourself or adapt to changing circumstances around you. As you do, you bring yourself closer and closer to the "yes" you are looking for.

We also learned that sometimes, persisting in business has to take a back seat to your health. We learned that ten years seems to be the magic number when it comes to overnight success stories, and that gentle patience is key. Some of the most renowned *moguls* faced hundreds of "no"s before they got their one, victorious "yes." That means we have no excuse to give up or give in when we are rejected.

Be bold and relentless

Being bold and relentless is directly related to being persistent and persevering. To be persistent, you often also have to be bold. We have to keep going, keep evolving, keep changing, keep adapting to feedback and criticism. We learned that we have to not embarrass easily. We have learned that fear MUST be overcome in order for our businesses to realize its full potential, that competition can be a source of fear, and that even underdogs have a chance at winning when they are bold and relentless.

Making and managing your mistakes

Making mistakes is just another part of the journey, when you are an entrepreneur. We learned that to help us manage our mistakes, we need a clear vision of what we want out of our resources, opportunities, and business relationships. Having that clear vision allows us to walk away from situations that might slow us down, use up our precious resources, or stop us from reaching our goals. We learned that it is important to know when to walk away from those harmful situations, and to be alert to red flags and proactive about acting on them. We learned that protecting our businesses through the use of reputable systems, and that contracts are always better than relying solely on trust, no matter what type of resource, opportunity, or business relationship we enter into.

Pursue Your Passions

Pursuing your passions is always the ideal when it comes to entrepreneurship. The two types of passions we discussed are personal passions, which you use to bring meaning and joy to your own life, and service-related passions, which we can use in the service of others. We learned that service-related passions are usually the best choices to drive our work in entrepreneurship.

We also reviewed two ways to find your passions. One is figuring out what frustrates you; the other is figuring out you would do for free. The second one, in particular, is useful for choosing what to organize your business around. We learned that when your work is the pursuit of your passion, you are less likely to burn out, more likely to persevere through obstacles, more likely to be more creative and inventive with your ideas, and more likely to work harder.

Finally, if there is a passion you want to pursue through business but that you do not quite have the skills for, we learned there are two good ways forward. You can pursue that passion by honing the skills in question through education, additional practice, and mentorship, or by hiring others who are skilled in the area in question.

The importance of your circle and network

We used the cliché "your network is your net worth" because there is a lot of truth to in it. We learned that protecting our energy is paramount for the success of our businesses. Our networks or often underutilized, and the type of network we invest in matters a great deal. We learned that it is easier to connect and utilize resources within an upwardly mobile network than it is to go head-hunting in an effort to build new networks. We learned that it is important to be connected to people who have worked in the area of business you hope to enter, because they often have priceless advice to offer. Look at me! I could have avoided a failed book project if I had only known my publishing mentor several months ahead of time. Seasoned advice is irreplaceable.

Self-care

I spent some additional time on the subject of self-care because it is so deeply important and so thoroughly neglected. Entrepreneurs often neglect this and find themselves unable to run their businesses as a result. Without maintaining their physical and mental health, they lack the energy, focus, and reserves to persevere when times get tough. Some tips for self-care are to rely on your faith; get plenty of exercise; eat, and eat right; take quiet time and practice meditation, spend time with friends and loved ones; build in moments to celebrate yourself and your achievements; and get proper sleep!

THANK YOU

We all have the capacity to become the next *mogul*, and if we make these moves for our businesses, we will be that much closer to doing so. Whether you are thinking about starting a business, are just starting out, or are a seasoned owner of multiple businesses, these are moves that anyone can make to immediately improve their entrepreneurial practice. Thank you for taking the time to read this book. I hope that it held everything that you were looking to learn, and more.

Be Bold. Be Relentless. Make Mogul Moves.

~Sharnae

Acknowledgments

I could not have imagined how much of a challenge it would be to write and finish this book. It took me eight months from start to finish, and in that time there were so many ups and downs. So many times I wanted quit, and almost let myself. So many times I second-guessed myself, and wondered whether I should be the person to relay this information. None of this would have been possible without my amazing support system.

I'm grateful for my family: my mother Charlotte; my father Angelo; my sisters Anzea, Alita-Geri, and Aschay; my nieces and nephews Jael, Joel, Israel, Reese, Naomi, and Alexander; my brothers in love, Jason and Ricardo; my grandmother Florence; and my aunt Geri. You all sacrificed phone conversations and quality time with me while I wrote this book. You were also there to encourage me, provide basic necessities for me when I needed them, and to always love me the ways I need to be loved most! Thanks for calling me every morning to check up on me. Thanks for Facetiming me with the babies. Thanks for volunteering your time, money, and resources to get help me through this past year and to get this business going the way I want it.

To Aaron (Judah) and Christa, I want you two to know that you can do ANYTHING you want to do. You can be what you want to be. I want you to know that you are smart, kind, and wonderful children and human beings who will make an amazing impact on the world. It is never too early to start dreaming, never too early to start your own business(es), never too early to be who you want to be.

To my wonderful friends, Melannie, Melinda, and Jarmone. You all knew how to keep me going. You knew when I needed a break to get away. When I needed to take care of myself. When I needed extra encouragement. When instead of burrowing down, I needed to come up for air. You all made sure I was not neglecting myself through this process. I often do so much, and have so much on my plate, and you all provided the comedic relief I needed and the break time necessary for me to recharge. Thank you for understanding when I could not make it to events, gatherings, and trips while I got this done. Thank you for letting me cry. For the hugs. Thank you all for knowing me the ways you do!

To my team, Crystal, Miriam, Alita-Geri, and Aunt Geri. You all are always down and ready to GO, WHENEVER I come up with a new idea. Whenever I want to put on a new workshop, teach a class, throw a book launch, or invent a product (yes, I know I can be a bit too ambitious sometimes), you all are always there to go on the ride with me and I am FOREVER grateful for your loyalty and time, and for the genuine love that you have for me. Not only are you my team, you are my family.

To my i5 City Church family: I love you all! Pastor Victor and Pastor Amby, Jessica, and Emmanuel, thank you for your support! Whether it was praying for me; reading an excerpt of the book; encouraging me through the process; or being a listening ear. The four of you made yourselves visible and available. I appreciate you.

To my boss ladies, Tressa 'Azarel' Smallwood, Jackie Hicks, and Renee Kelly. Thank you. You all have all played major parts in this book. Whether it was through an introduction, shepherding me through the publishing process, or helping me to do this marketing thing the RIGHT way, you have helped me tremendously. Thank you for believing in me and giving me the confidence that I CAN DO THIS!

Most importantly, to my Lord. Above all else and all things, thank you for being all who you are, and all that you are. Thank you for bringing me this far. Thank you for trusting me. Thank you for your spirit that guides me every day, that gives me the ability and intelligence to have written this book in the first place. Thank you for the certainty that there is so much more in store that we will accomplish as a team. Thank you for ALWAYS, ALWAYS, making things work for me, even when I feel like a failure.

Here's to many more journeys and adventures.

~Sharnae

Made in the USA
San Bernardino, CA
04 November 2018